Paella Cookbook

Timeless Paella Recipes for the Family

By
BookSumo Press
All rights reserved

Published by
http://www.booksumo.com

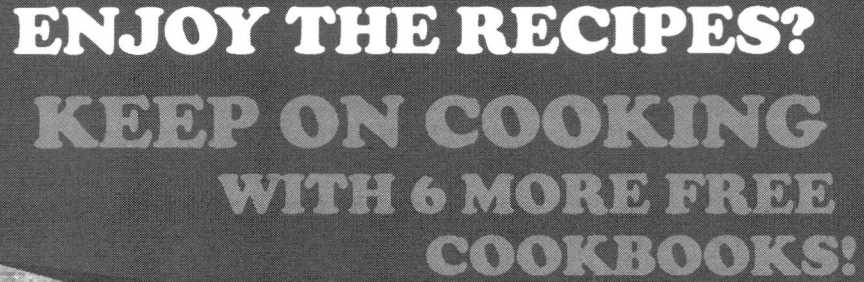

ENJOY THE RECIPES?
KEEP ON COOKING WITH 6 MORE FREE COOKBOOKS!

Visit our website and simply enter your email address to join the club and receive your 6 cookbooks.

http://booksumo.com/magnet

https://www.instagram.com/booksumopress/

https://www.facebook.com/booksumo/

LEGAL NOTES

All Rights Reserved. No Part Of This Book May Be Reproduced Or Transmitted In Any Form Or By Any Means. Photocopying, Posting Online, And / Or Digital Copying Is Strictly Prohibited Unless Written Permission Is Granted By The Book's Publishing Company. Limited Use Of The Book's Text Is Permitted For Use In Reviews Written For The Public.

Table of Contents

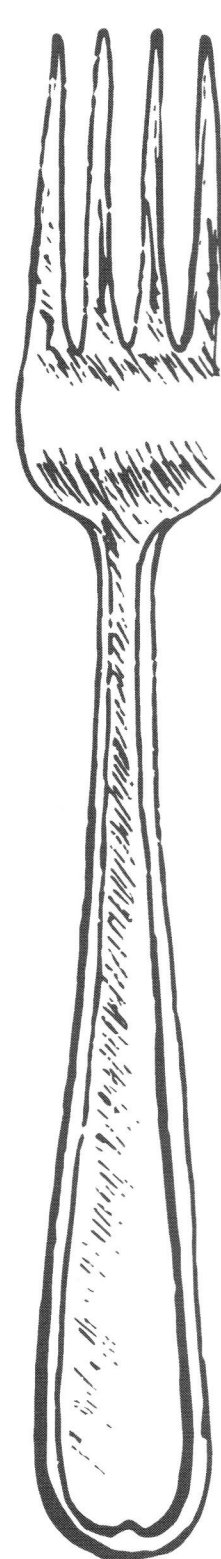

Guyanese Paella 9

Traditional Paella in Portuguese Style 10

2 Brother's Paella 11

Cajun Paella 12

Butter Bean Paella 13

Beacon Hill Paella 14

Italian Paella 15

Paella Maella 16

American Paella 17

Vegan One Pot Dinner 18

30-Minute Wednesday Paella 19

Central America Paella 20

Paella Rustica 21

Paella Trinidad 22

Florentine Paella 23

Paella Cutlets 24

Florentine Paella 25

Baby Paella 26

Milanese Paella 27

Golden Paella 28

Riverside Paella 29

Southwest Paella 30

Paella Calamari 31

Honey Saffron Paella 32

Sweet Mexicana Paella 33

Roasted Paella 34

Chicken and Chorizo Paella 35

Paella Estrellita 36

Paella Winters 37

Paella Summers 38

White and Brown Rice Paella 40

Portuguese Pan 41

Our Best Paella 42

Paella Zaragoza 43

Polish Paella 44

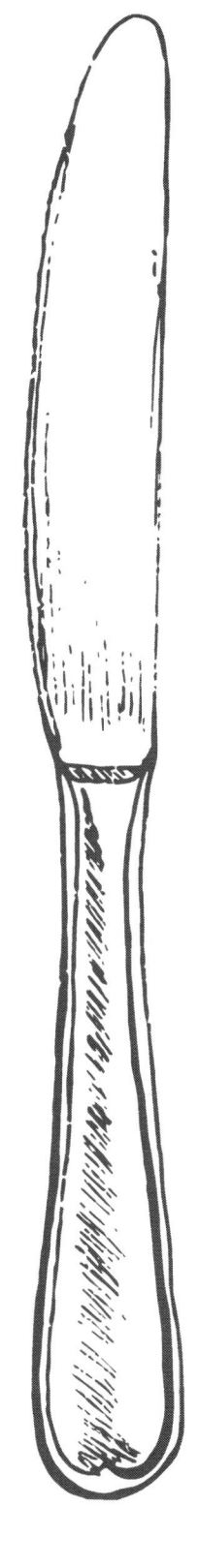

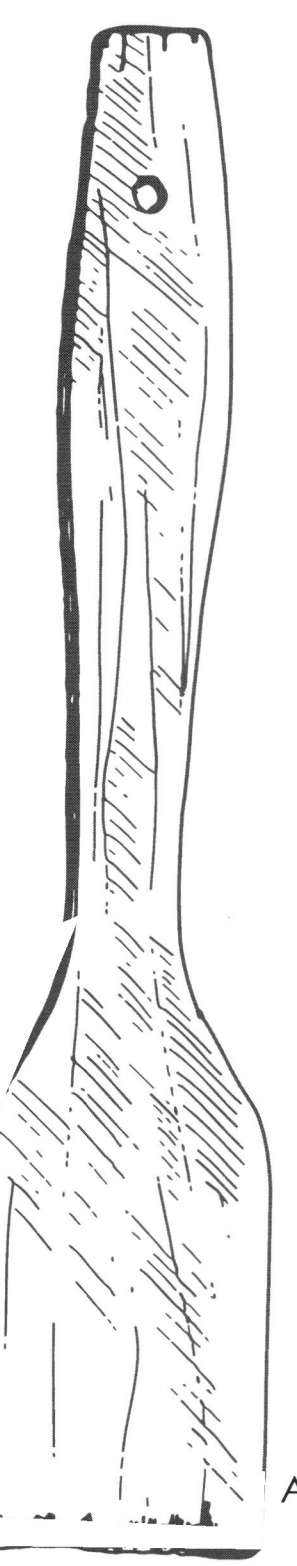

City Park Paella 45

New England Paella 46

Sun Dried Parmesan Paella 47

Southern Barcelona Paella 48

Weekend Paella 49

Classical One-Pot Hot Pot 50

Stunning Paella 51

Paella in Mediterranean Style 52

Classico Paella 53

Summer Veggie Paella 54

Paella Forever 55

Grand Theft Paella 56

Restaurant Style Paella 57

Swedish Paella 58

Paella for Celebrations 59

Mountain-Style Paella 60

Rich Paella 62

Authentic Seafood Paella in Spanish Style 63

Midweek Paella 64

Distinctive Paella 65

Mexican Paella 66

Incredibly Delicious Paella 67

Gourmet Dinner Paella 69

Island Chicken Paella 70

South African Style Paella 71

Persian Paella 72

Innovative Paella 73

Paella for Parties 74

Italian Paella 75

Paleo Paella 76

Paella in Barcelona Style 77

Denver Style Paella 78

Fiesta Paella 79

Nutritious Paella 80

Hearty Paella 81

Paella in Vegan Style 82

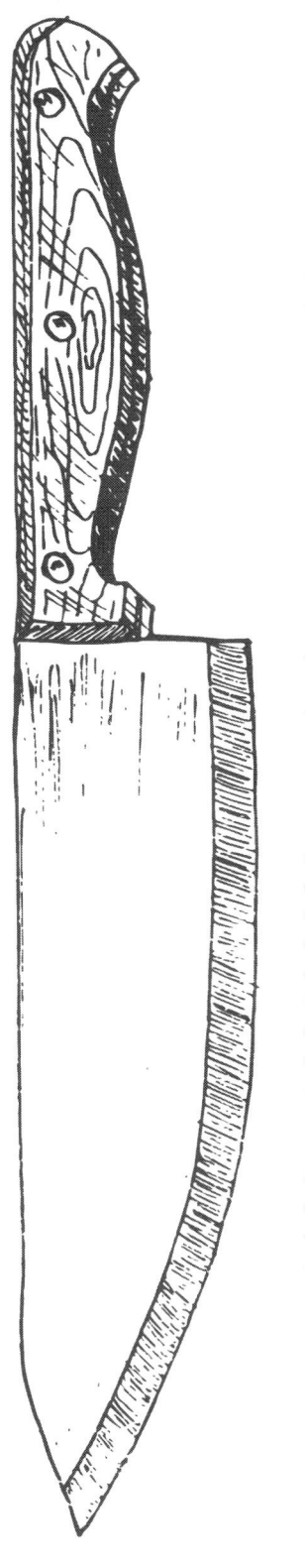

Family Friendly Paella 84

Flavor-Packed Paella 85

Versatile Paella 86

Traditional Restaurant Style Paella 87

Comfort brown Rice Paella 88

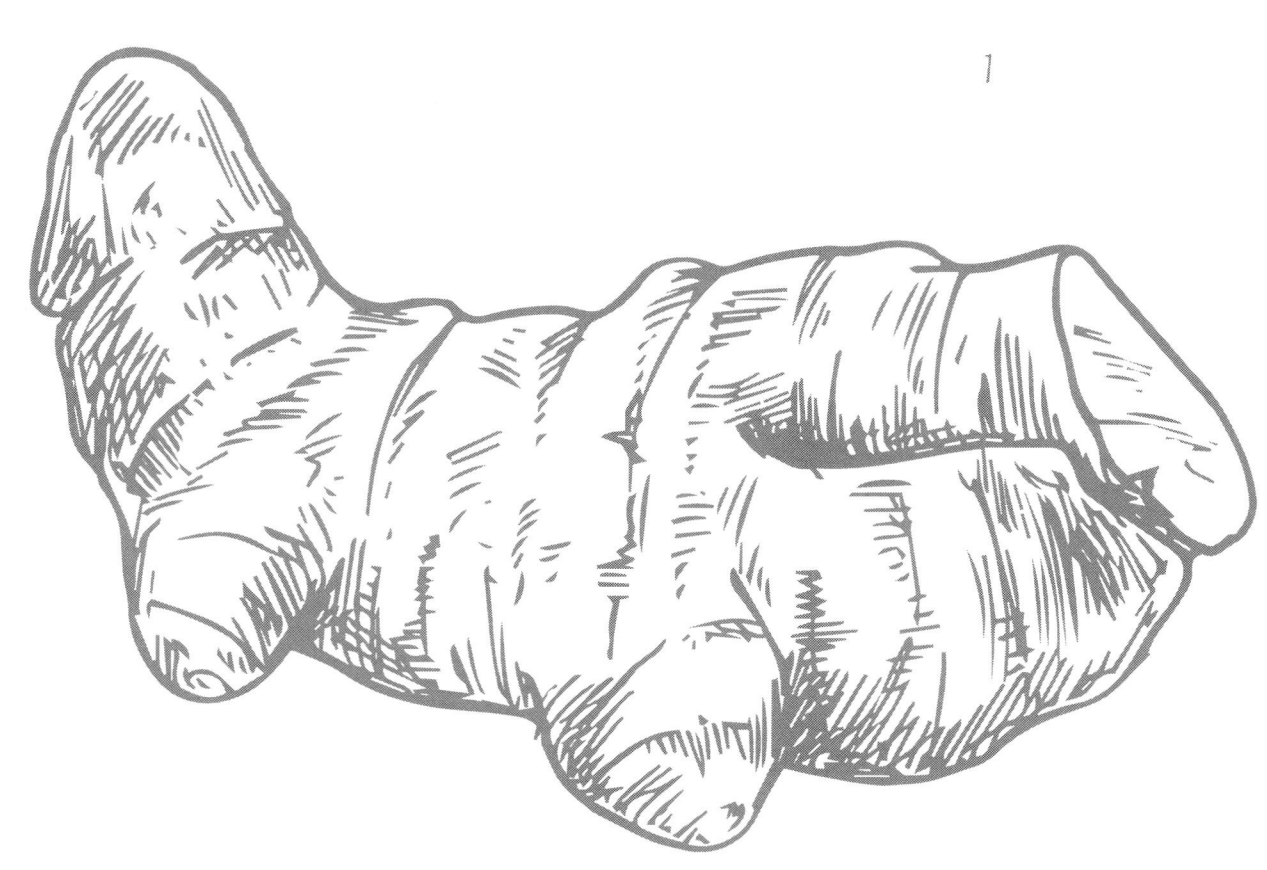

Guyanese Paella

Prep Time: 20 mins
Total Time: 50 mins

Servings per Recipe: 4
Calories   555.9
Fat   15.0g
Cholesterol   139.4mg
Sodium   860.0mg
Carbohydrates   61.0g
Protein   42.1g

Ingredients

- 2 tsps. sesame oil
- 125 g shallots, peeled and sliced
- 20 g gingerroot, grated
- 2 garlic cloves, chopped
- 400 g chicken breasts
- salt and pepper
- 250 g orzo pasta
- 1 1/2 tsps. smoked paprika
- 600 ml chicken stock
- 225 - 250 g prawns, cooked
- 1/4 C. lemon juice
- 3 tsps. soy sauce
- 1/3 C. coriander leaves, chopped

Directions

1. Slice the chicken into 3cm pieces.
2. Pour sesame oil into a skillet and heat well.
3. Sauté shallots, garlic and ginger until soft for a few minutes.
4. Toss in the chicken pieces to the skillet, adjust seasonings by adding salt and pepper and cook until nicely browned on each side.
5. Stir in orzo and allow to coat with sesame oil.
6. Adjust seasonings with paprika and pour the stock over the ingredients. All the stock may not be required at once.
7. Leave to simmer for about 16 minutes. Add more stock if necessary.
8. Stir in the prawns, soy and lemon juice and combine well. Adjust seasonings if required.
9. Leave for 6 minutes in the skillet, cover and allow the chicken to become tender.
10. Add the chopped coriander and serve with more leaves.
11. Enjoy.

TRADITIONAL
Paella in Portuguese Style

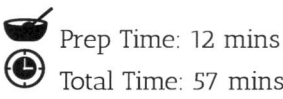 Prep Time: 12 mins
Total Time: 57 mins

Servings per Recipe: 6
Calories 607.4
Fat 18.4g
Cholesterol 193.6mg
Sodium 1314.2mg
Carbohydrates 65.4g
Protein 42.0g

Ingredients

1/4 C. olive oil
3 chicken breasts, cubed
1/2 tsp. salt
1/4 tsp. pepper
1 large Spanish onion, chopped
1 green pepper, diced into pieces
4 cloves garlic, chopped
2 tsps. Spanish paprika
1 tbsp. fresh thyme
1 lb. shrimp, shelled and deveined
2 C. Arborio rice
1 C. chopped tomatoes
5 C. chicken broth
1/2 tsp. saffron thread
1 C. lima beans
1/2 C. roasted red pepper, strips
1/4 C. chopped parsley
12 clams in shell
lemon wedge
green onion

Directions

1. Pour 3 tbsp oil into a pan and heat well.
2. Toss in the chicken and sauté for 5 minutes on each side until a slight brown in color.
3. Transfer the chicken into a dish and adjust seasonings with salt and pepper.
4. Fold in peppers and onions into the pan and temper for 3 minutes.
5. Add paprika, garlic and thyme and leave for 1 minute.
6. Toss in shrimp and leave until pink in color.
7. Pour 1 tbsp oil if required.
8. Add rice into the pan; stir and temper for 4 minutes until evenly coated in oil.
9. Add the tomatoes.
10. Pour the saffron and stock into the rice mixture and allow the mixture to boil for 3 minutes.
11. Lower the heat to medium.
12. Transfer the chicken once again into the pan with rice.
13. Remove lid and leave to cook for 16 minutes.
14. Allow the mixture to bubble.
15. Add lima beans, shrimp, clams and red peppers and cook for 12 minutes.
16. Transfer from heat and keep covered for 12 minutes.
17. Sprinkle parsley on top and serve garnished with green onions and lemon wedges.
18. Enjoy.

2 Brother's Paella

🥣 Prep Time: 1 hr
🕐 Total Time: 1 hr 45 mins

Servings per Recipe: 8
Calories   887.3
Fat   28.6g
Cholesterol   344.9mg
Sodium   1820.9mg
Carbohydrates   76.8g
Protein   74.1g

Ingredients

2 1/2 lbs. chicken parts
1/4 C. olive oil
1 medium onion, diced
4 garlic cloves, minced
2 tsps. salt
ground pepper
1/2 tsp. paprika
1 large red bell pepper, roasted, peeled, seeded, and diced
1/2 C. sliced green onion
1 lb. squid, cleaned, sacs cut into rings
1/2 tsp. saffron thread
1 lb. large raw shrimp, peeled and deveined
3 C. short-grain rice
6 C. warm chicken stock
1 1/2 lbs. small live clams
1 C. frozen peas

Directions

1. Slice each breast half into 3 parts and each thigh into 4 parts.
2. Pour the oil into a skillet and heat well.
3. Sauté the onion and garlic for a few minutes.
4. Increase the heat when the onions begin to sizzle.
5. Stir in the chicken and allow to cook until slightly browned; sprinkle paprika, salt and pepper on the chicken.
6. Once the chicken is cooked transfer the pieces towards the outside of the skillet making room in the middle of the skillet.
7. Stir in the squid, green onion, peppers and the balance salt; crumble the saffron and add to the chicken. Fold in the rice and leave for 2 minutes to coat evenly with oil.
8. Pour the hot stock to within 1" of the rim of the skillet. You may not require all the stock.
9. Spread the shrimp on top; place the clams and mussels in a circle around the edge, hinged side facing downwards.
10. Allow the mixture to simmer for about 22 minutes until the rice becomes tender; sprinkle the peas on top midway during the cooking time. Enjoy.

CAJUN
Paella

Prep Time: 1 hr 30 mins
Total Time: 2 hr

Servings per Recipe: 8
Calories 809.6
Fat 47.1g
Cholesterol 235.1mg
Sodium 1305.5mg
Carbohydrates 40.1g
Protein 52.0g

Ingredients

1/4 C. olive oil
3 lbs. chicken, cut-up, bone-in
1/4 C. water
1 tsp. oregano
1 large onion, chopped
2 garlic cloves, minced
1/2 tbsp. parsley, minced
1 seeded jalapeno, minced
2 C. long-grain rice
1/2 tsp. turmeric

3 tbsp. butter
4 C. chicken broth
scant 1/2 tsp. salt
1 lb. shrimp, cooked and cleaned
1/2 lb. smoked sausage, sliced
1/4 lb. ham, diced, optional
salt and pepper

Directions

1. Rub the chicken with salt and pepper.
2. Pour olive oil into a skillet and heat well; toss in the chicken and keep until a slight brown in color.
3. Stir in oregano and 1/4 C. water; cover with lid and leave for 35 minutes until the chicken becomes tender.
4. Take out the cooked chicken and leave aside.
5. Add the onion and garlic to the skillet and sauté until soft. Add the jalapeno and the parsley.
6. Heat the butter and allow to melt in a separate saucepan with lid; cover and leave on a low heat for 18 minutes.
7. Stir in garlic and onion and combine well.
8. Arrange the rice, shrimp, chicken, ham and sausage in layers in an ovenproof dish. Bake for 32 minutes at a temperature of 350F. Enjoy.

Butter Bean Paella

Prep Time: 30 mins
Total Time: 2 hrs

Servings per Recipe: 8
Calories	31.3
Fat	82
Cholesterol	328
Sodium	87.3
Carbohydrates	34.2
Protein	31.3

Ingredients

1 tbsp. olive oil
1/2 (4 pound) whole chicken, cut into 6 pieces
1/2 (2 pound) rabbit, cleaned and cut into pieces
1 head garlic, cloves separated and peeled
1 tomato, chopped
1 (15.5 ounce) can butter beans
1/2 (10 ounce) package frozen green peas
1/2 (10 ounce) package frozen green beans
salt
1 tsp. mild paprika
1 pinch saffron threads
dried thyme
dried rosemary
4 C. uncooked white rice

Directions

1. Pour olive oil into a skillet and heat well. Toss in the rabbit, chicken and garlic and cook until a slight brown in color. Transfer the slightly browned meat into a side of the skillet; add tomato, peas and butter beans. Adjust seasonings with paprika and combine the mixture well.
2. Measure the water and pour into the skillet. Allow the mixture to boil, reduce heat and allow the mixture to simmer for about 1 hour and 10 minutes.
3. Add a pinch of salt and saffron for color yellow. If required add rosemary and thyme.
4. Fold in the rice, cover with lid, lower the heat and allow the mixture to simmer until the liquid dries up for about 22 minutes.
5. Enjoy.

BEACON
Hill Paella

🥣 Prep Time: 45 mins
🕐 Total Time: 1 hr 15 mins

Servings per Recipe: 8
Calories   290.3
Fat   4.5g
Cholesterol   21.7mg
Sodium   220.5mg
Carbohydrates   47.6g
Protein   13.8g

Ingredients

1 white onion, medium dice
1 red bell pepper, medium dice
2 C. long grain rice
2 - 3 sausage links, cut across into rounds
1 (8 ounce) packages chicken tenders, cut across into pieces
15 - 20 medium shrimp, cleaned, uncooked
3 green onions, sliced across
1 C. frozen peas, steamed, drained
1 (32 ounce) boxes chicken stock
1 bay leaf
1 tbsp. saffron
2 - 3 garlic cloves, chopped
2 tsps. red pepper flakes
1 tbsp. paprika
1 - 3 tbsp. olive oil
1 - 2 tsp. salt and pepper
1 lemon wedges

Directions

1. Add the bay leaf and saffron into a saucepan and pour in the chicken stock. Allow the mixture to simmer.
2. Rub the chicken with salt, pepper and paprika.
3. Pour 1 1/2 tbsp olive oil into a skillet and temper the chicken until a slight brown on all sides. Remove the ingredients and transfer into a platter.
4. Toss in sausage to the skillet and allow to brown on all sides. Combine the sausage with the chicken whilst keeping any oil in the skillet.
5. Toss in onion, garlic, red bell pepper, salt and pepper into the skillet and temper for a few minutes until soft. Add more oil if required.
6. Stir in the rice and stir fry for 5 minutes.
7. Pour the chicken stock to the skillet, combine, lower the heat, cover with lid and allow to simmer for 12 minutes.
8. Add the chicken, shrimp and sausage. Sprinkle peas on top, keep the lid on and allow the mixture to simmer for 12 more minutes.
9. Transfer from heat, sprinkle green onions on top.
10. Serve with wedges of lemon.
11. Enjoy.

Italian Paella

Prep Time: 5 mins
Total Time: 30 mins

Servings per Recipe: 5
Calories   603.9
Fat   12.8g
Cholesterol   351.8mg
Sodium   850.3mg
Carbohydrates   74.6g
Protein   43.2g

Ingredients

- 1 lb. shrimp
- 1 lb. squid
- 1 lb. mussels
- 2 C. short-grain rice
- 1 onion, minced
- 1 tbsp. tomato paste
- 1/2 green pepper
- 1/2 red pepper
- 2 garlic cloves, minced
- 3 tbsp. olive oil
- 1/2 tsp. saffron thread
- salt
- pepper
- 5 C. water

Directions

1. Pour olive oil into a skillet and heat well. Sauté the onion and garlic for 4 minutes.
2. Toss in the tomato paste and peppers and leave for 4 more minutes.
3. Stir in the rice, squids, saffron, salt and pepper and leave for 4 minutes.
4. Pour the warm water into the ingredients.
5. Stir in the balance olive oil.
6. Once the liquid is absorbed stir in the mussels and shrimps.
7. Stir occasionally and allow to cook for 12 more minutes.
8. Enjoy.

PAELLA
Maella

Prep Time: 10 mins
Total Time: 55 mins

Servings per Recipe: 4
Calories   412.4
Fat   11.6g
Cholesterol   0.0mg
Sodium   1202.0mg
Carbohydrates   71.5g
Protein   8.3g

Ingredients

3 tbsp. olive oil
1 large onion, diced
6 garlic cloves, minced
1/2 tsp. red chili pepper flakes
2 tsps. salt
1 tbsp. chili powder
1 tbsp. sweet paprika
2 tsps. oregano
1 large red pepper, chopped
1 large yellow pepper, chopped
4 medium tomatoes, ripe, chopped

1 1/4 C. Arborio rice
3 C. vegetable stock
1/2 lb. green beans, trimmed and sliced into lengths
fresh ground pepper
1/2 bunch cilantro, chopped
1/2 bunch parsley, chopped
1 bunch scallion, minced
cheddar cheese

Directions

1. Pour olive oil into a skillet and heat well. Add onion and allow to cook until tender. Toss in chile flakes, garlic and 1 tsp salt and temper until the garlic becomes soft.
2. Stir in the balance salt, herbs, spices, tomatoes and peppers, cover with lid and allow to simmer for 12 minutes. Add the rice and allow to coat evenly.
3. Pour the water or stock to a saucepan, heat and pour the warm liquid into the skillet. Cover with lid and lower the heat.
4. Allow the rice to cook until tender for 32 minutes until the liquid has been fully absorbed. In the meantime, blanch or steam the beans until soft.
5. Stir in the beans to the skillet. Adjust seasonings with fresh herbs and cracked pepper.
6. Garnish with minced scallions and grated cheese and serve.
7. Enjoy.

American Paella

 Prep Time: 15 mins
 Total Time: 55 mins

Servings per Recipe: 6
Calories   752.8
Fat   33.8g
Cholesterol   214.0mg
Sodium   1643.0mg
Carbohydrates   65.8g
Protein   44.2g

Ingredients

1 tbsp. olive oil
1 lb. chorizo sausage, sliced
1 large onion, diced
2 garlic cloves, minced
1 (1 ounce) packet vegetable soup mix
1/2 tsp. paprika
2 C. long-grain rice
4 C. low sodium chicken broth
1 (14 ounce) cans diced tomatoes, drained

1 C. frozen peas
1 lb. previously cooked frozen shrimp
pepper

Directions

1. Before you do anything set the oven to 400F. Pour oil into a skillet and heat well. Sauté the chorizo and leave for 6 minutes until a slight brown in color. Toss in onion and garlic and leave for 3 minutes.
2. Add the rice, soup mix and paprika; allow the rice to coat with soup mix and leave for 2 minutes.
3. Add the broth and allow the mixture to boil. Add the tomatoes and allow the mixture to simmer. Cover with lid.
4. Place the dish in the oven and bake for 16 minutes. Add shrimp and peas and cook for 6 more minutes. Transfer from oven and allow to rest for 12 minutes prior to removing the cover. With the use of a fork fluff the rice and adjust seasonings with pepper. Serve warm.
5. Enjoy.

VEGAN
One Pot Dinner

Prep Time: 30 mins
Total Time: 1 hr 10 mins

Servings per Recipe: 8
Calories   260.1
Fat   6.7g
Cholesterol   0.0mg
Sodium   461.2mg
Carbohydrates   45.5g
Protein   6.6g

Ingredients

1 pinch saffron
1 medium eggplant, cut into chunks
3 tbsp. extra virgin olive oil
1 yellow onion, chopped
5 garlic cloves, crushed
1 yellow pepper, chopped
1 red bell pepper, chopped
1 tsp. dried cilantro
2 tsps. sweet Spanish paprika
1 C. Arborio rice
3 1/2 C. vegetable broth
1 (15 ounce) cans diced tomatoes
1/2 tsp. cayenne powder
1/2 tsp. sea salt
1 tsp. dried thyme
ground black pepper
1 C. mushroom, sliced
1 C. green beans, cut into thirds
1 (15 ounce) cans chickpeas, rinsed and drained
1/4 C. pitted black olives, sliced
1 tbsp. parsley, minced

Directions

1. Pour 3 tbsp of water over saffron in a bowl and leave aside. Sprinkle salt on eggplant pieces and place in a colander for 35 minutes. Rinse the pieces and drain with the use of a colander.
2. Pour olive oil into a skillet and heat well. Toss in the onion, cilantro, garlic, eggplant and peppers and sauté for 6 minutes. Sprinkle paprika and combine the ingredients well. Stir in the rice, tomatoes, saffron water, vegetable stock, cayenne, salt, thyme and ground black pepper. Allow the mixture to boil, lower the heat and allow to simmer. Cook uncovered for 16 minutes. Combine well.
3. Toss in the mushrooms, chickpeas and green beans. Cook without a lid ensuring to stir often and leave for another 16 minutes until the rice becomes tender and the sauce becomes thick in consistency. To keep the rice moist more broth, white wine or water may be added as required.
4. Increase the heat to high for 6 minutes until the bottom forms a caramelized crust. Check the crust with the use of a fork, ensuring not to burn the rice. Remove from heat and allow to sit for 6 minutes. Garnish with olive slices and fresh parsley and serve warm.
5. Enjoy.

30-Minute Wednesday Paella

Prep Time: 10 mins
Total Time: 30mins

Servings per Recipe: 6
Calories   220.3
Fat   9.4g
Cholesterol   101.3mg
Sodium   445.2mg
Carbohydrates   10.9g
Protein   22.6g

Ingredients

- 3 C. quick-cooking brown rice
- 1 C. frozen peas
- 1 tbsp. olive oil
- 2 chicken breasts, of approx. 4oz each diced
- 1 medium yellow onion, chopped
- 2 garlic cloves, minced
- 4 ounces fully cooked smoked turkey sausage, sliced
- 1 (15 ounce) cans crushed tomatoes
- 1/4 tsp. saffron thread
- 1/4 tsp. turmeric
- 1/4 tsp. paprika
- 1/4-1/2 tsp. hot seasoning sauce
- 8 ounces medium shrimp, peeled and deveined

Directions

1. Cook the brown rice as per package instructions. Transfer the rice from the heat, stir in the peas, cover with lid and allow to stand for 6 minutes.
2. Pour oil into a pan and heat well. Sauté the chicken until cooked; take out from the heat and leave aside.
3. Toss in onion and garlic and leave for 4 minutes until soft.
4. Stir in the sausage into the pan and allow to heat through.
5. Add tomatoes, seasonings and spices and allow the mixture to simmer. Toss in the shrimp, cover with lid and cook for 4 minutes until shrimp is pink in color.
6. Fold in the brown rice and chicken.
7. Enjoy.

CENTRAL American Paella (Belizean Inspired)

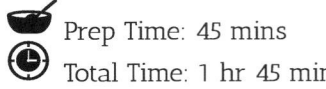

Prep Time: 45 mins
Total Time: 1 hr 45 mins

Servings per Recipe: 6
Calories 393.2
Fat 11.0g
Cholesterol 26.1mg
Sodium 539.4mg
Carbohydrates 51.9g
Protein 21.5g

Ingredients

1/4 C. olive oil
16 ounces scallops
1 large onion, chopped
2 garlic cloves, minced
1 1/2 C. rice
3 1/4 C. fish stock
1/4 tsp. saffron
salt and pepper
1 red bell pepper, roasted and cut in strips
18 mild green canned chilies
1 (14 ounce) cans artichoke hearts, drained and sprinkled with lemon juice
lemon wedge

Directions

1. Pour half the quantity of olive oil into a skillet and heat well. Toss in the scallops and temper for 4 minutes. Transfer the scallops to a dish and dispose the pan juices.
2. Pour the balance olive oil into the skillet and sauté the onion and garlic for 6 minutes. Stir in the rice and allow to cook for 6 more minutes. Fold in the saffron, broth, salt and pepper and leave to cook for 12 minutes. Stir in the chilies and roasted red bell peppers and allow to cook for another 12 minutes. Fold in the artichoke hearts and fried scallops and allow to cook for 6 minutes until the liquid has been fully absorbed and the rice is soft and tender.
3. Serve garnished with wedges of lemon or additional roasted sweet red bell pepper strips. Serve warm.
4. Enjoy.

Paella Rustica

🥣 Prep Time: 45 mins
🕐 Total Time: 1 hr 45 mins

Servings per Recipe: 4
Calories   1504.0
Fat   69.5g
Cholesterol   340.1mg
Sodium   329.8mg
Carbohydrates   115.2g
Protein   96.6g

Ingredients

- 4 - 8 chicken
- 2 onions, chopped
- 1 - 3 garlic clove, chopped
- 1 tsp. turmeric
- 115 - 250 g chorizo sausage, cooked
- 250 g rice
- 1 liter stock
- 4 tomatoes, peeled and chopped
- 1 red pepper
- 1 C. peas
- salt and pepper

Directions

1. Rub paprika on the chicken and place the chicken in a skillet and leave until nicely browned. Transfer the chicken to a side of the skillet.
2. Sauté the onions for a few minutes.
3. Stir in the garlic and turmeric and allow to cook for a few minutes.
4. Toss in the chorizo and stir fry for a few minutes.
5. Fold in rice and half the quantity of stock. If you prefer a spicy paella add balsamic/lee, red wine/sherry and Perrins etc.
6. Stir in the peppers, tomato and vegetables.
7. Place on the hob until the rice is done, add stock as required.
8. Sprinkle parsley, bacon and peppers on top.
9. Serve garnished with white wine and French or Spanish bread.
10. Enjoy.

PAELLA
Trinidad

Prep Time: 10 mins
Total Time: 1 hr 10 mins

Servings per Recipe: 8
Calories 462.6
Fat 17.1g
Cholesterol 121.9mg
Sodium 1008.7mg
Carbohydrates 44.5g
Protein 28.3g

Ingredients

1 lb. large shrimp, peeled and deveined
1 green bell pepper, seeded and sliced into strips
3 chicken breasts, strips
3 smoked sausage, sliced
1 large onion, chopped
1 (14 1/2 ounce) cans diced tomatoes, undrained
2 C. sweet rice
3 C. chicken broth
1/3 C. dry red wine
1/2 tsp. saffron thread
1 piece bay leaf
1/2 tsp. salt
1/2 C. frozen peas, thawed
1/2 C. seafood
2 tbsp. oil

Directions

1. Marinate the shrimps with ¼ tsp salt, 1 tsp minced garlic, ¼ tsp black pepper, 1 tbsp oil and ½ tsp Old Bay seasoning. Use a plastic wrap to cover and leave in the refrigerator.
2. Pour oil into a skillet and sauté the strips of green bell pepper, remove to a bowl and leave aside. Pour additional oil and sauté the chicken breast for 4 minutes per side. Place the cooked chicken towards the sides of the skillet, and stir in chorizos or smoked sausages into the skillet. Allow the chorizos to brown for about 5 minutes. Remove the chicken and chorizo to a platter and leave aside.
3. Pour 2 tbsp of oil into the skillet and stir fry the onions until soft. Toss in the tomatoes along with the juice and 2 C. of rice and combine well until the tomato mixture coats the sweet rice.
4. Pour chicken broth and wine over the ingredients. Add bay leaf, saffron threads and cooked chorizos and chicken and allow the mixture to boil. Stir once in a while.
5. Transfer the mixture to a baking dish, cover with lid and leave in the oven for 22 minutes at a temperature of 350F until the rice is done and the mixture becomes dry. Remove lid and arrange the shrimp, bell peppers and seafood mix. Cover with lid and place back again in the oven and bake for 16 minutes. Take out from the oven and allow the mixture to stand for 6 minutes.
6. Enjoy.

Florentine Paella

Prep Time: 10 mins
Total Time: 40 mins

Servings per Recipe: 4
Calories 551.8
Fat 14.4g
Cholesterol 0.0mg
Sodium 47.8mg
Carbohydrates 91.1g
Protein 8.6g

Ingredients

- 3 C. water
- 1/2 C. white wine
- 1 1/2 lbs. ripe tomatoes, cored and cut into wedges
- salt & ground black pepper
- 1/4 C. extra virgin olive oil
- 1 medium onion, minced
- 1 tbsp. minced garlic
- 1 tbsp. tomato paste
- 1 pinch saffron thread
- 1 - 2 tsp. paprika
- 2 C. short-grain rice
- minced parsley, and basil

Directions

1. Before you do anything set the oven to 450F. Pour water into a pot and heat well. Place the tomatoes in a bowl, sprinkle salt and pepper on top and pour 1 tbsp of olive oil on the tomatoes. Allow to coat well.
2. Pour the balance oil in an ovenproof dish. Sauté onion and garlic and add salt to the pan and cook for 6 minutes until the veggies are soft. Pour tomato paste, paprika and saffron and cook for 2 more minutes. Fold in the rice and cook for 3 minutes. Pour wine and allow to simmer until the mixture is dry, then fold in the warm water and combine well.
3. Arrange wedges of tomato on the rice and drizzle the juices from the bowl on top. Place the ovenproof dish in the oven and leave for 16 minutes. If the rice is still uncooked place the pan once again in the oven and cook for further 12 minutes. If the rice is too dry add more stock or water. Once the rice is cooked switch off the oven and allow the dish to stand for 16 minutes. Take out the pan from oven, sprinkle basil and parsley on top.
4. Enjoy..

PAELLA
Cutlets

Prep Time: 25 mins
Total Time: 55 mins

Servings per Recipe: 1
Calories   108.6
Fat   4.8g
Cholesterol   32.3mg
Sodium   385.2mg
Carbohydrates   9.9g
Protein   5.8g

Ingredients

2 1/2 C. risotto rice
1 large onion, medium chopped
1 bay leaf
2 tsps. crushed garlic
1 chicken bouillon cube
1 1/2 tsps. saffron, crushed
1 tbsp. olive oil
5 C. chicken stock, heated
6 ounces salami
6 ounces smoked ham

seasoned flour
2 eggs, beaten with a little milk
seasoned dry breadcrumb
oil
parsley

Directions

1. Place rice in a saucepan. Add bay leaf, bouillon cube, olive oil, saffron/turmeric and garlic. Stir in hot water/stock into the saucepan. Allow the mixture to boil. Reduce the heat and allow to simmer for about 18 minutes until the liquid is fully absorbed.
2. Take out from the heat; discard the bay leaf and allow the mixture to cool in the room temperature.
3. Place the meats in a food processor, mince and add onto the rice mix. Form balls out of the mixture, if the mixture is too moist fold in bread crumbs or a bit of flour.
4. Roll the balls in seasoned flour until fully covered.
5. Dip them in the egg whip and then roll on breadcrumbs.
6. Leave overnight in the refrigerator.
7. Deep fry the balls in oil at a temperature of 365F until crispy and golden in color.
8. Sprinkle parsley on top and serve.
9. Enjoy.

Paella Confetti

Prep Time: 30 mins
Total Time: 1 hr

Servings per Recipe: 4
Calories	345.4
Fat	19.6g
Cholesterol	97.8mg
Sodium	760.6mg
Carbohydrates	22.0g
Protein	20.3g

Ingredients

- 1 large cauliflower
- 2 tbsp. olive oil
- 1 onion, diced
- 1 red bell pepper, diced
- 1 yellow bell pepper, diced
- 4 garlic cloves, minced
- 1 tsp. paprika
- 2 pinches saffron threads
- 1/2 lemon juice, and zest
- 1/4 C. dry white wine
- 2 Spanish chorizo sausages, sliced
- 1/2 lb. shrimp, deveined
- 1/4 C. parsley, chopped

Directions

1. Chop the cauliflower into small florets and place in a food processor. Process until it forms the consistency of grain and leave aside.
2. Pour oil into a pan and heat well. Toss in onion and temper until soft. Stir in the garlic and bell pepper and leave until slightly browned. Add the cauliflower, spices, white wine and stock or paella base. Fold in ham and chorizo and leave for about 6 minutes. If chorizo needs further cooking leave for additional 12 minutes.
3. Stir in shrimp and parsley and leave until the shrimp turns pink in color.
4. Serve warm.
5. Enjoy.

Florentine Paella

BABY
Paella

🍳 Prep Time: 20 mins
🕐 Total Time: 45 mins

Servings per Recipe: 4
Calories   702.4
Fat   24.8g
Cholesterol   218.0mg
Sodium   1918.2mg
Carbohydrates   70.5g
Protein   45.6g

Ingredients

1 whole chicken breasts, boned
1/4 lb. chicken livers
1/4 lb. lean pork, diced
1/4 C. olive oil
1 garlic clove, minced
1 pimiento, drained and diced
1 tomatoes, peeled and chopped
4 ounces frozen baby lima beans
1 1/2 C. rice
2 3/4 C. broth

1 1/2 tsps. salt
1/4 tsp. saffron
7 - 8 ounces clams
4 1/2 ounces large shrimp

Directions

1. Slice the chicken into 1" chunks. Pour olive oil into a skillet and sauté the pork and chicken livers until a light brown in color.
2. Toss in pimiento, garlic and tomato and cook for 2 minutes. Stir in the defrosted limas and rice and allow to coat evenly with oil.
3. Mix saffron with broth or water, add clams and juice and allow the mixture to boil. Pour the hot liquid over the rice.
4. Allow the mixture to boil and leave for 17 minutes. Toss in shrimp, cover with lid and maintain the warmth or place in a hot oven of 300F.
5. Leave for 12 minutes until the rice is tender and fluffy.
6. Enjoy.

Milanese Paella

Prep Time: 15 mins
Total Time: 15 mins

Servings per Recipe: 4
Calories	645.2
Fat	17.1g
Cholesterol	105.6mg
Sodium	889.2mg
Carbohydrates	91.3g
Protein	29.7g

Ingredients

- 4 C. fish stock
- 2 tsps. sweet smoked paprika
- 1 pinch salt
- 1/4-1/2 C. extra virgin olive oil
- 2 small lobsters, split in half
- 1 1/2 large brown onions, peeled & diced
- 1 red bell pepper, seeds & stem removed, chopped
- 3 garlic cloves, peeled & minced
- 2 C. Arborio rice
- 1 dozen small clam, scrubbed
- 2 fillets, white fish fillets cut into pieces
- 2 tbsp. parsley, chopped
- 2 lemons wedges

Directions

1. Place fish broth, salt and pimenton in a saucepan and heat on a low flame. In the meantime, pour the olive oil into a skillet and heat until almost smoking on a barbeque.
2. Toss in the prawns, flip once in a while and allow to cook for 8 minutes until a slight brown in color. Transfer the prawns to a platter and toss in the lobsters to the skillet, with shell side facing downwards and cook for 5 minutes, turn on the other side and leave for further 5 minutes.
3. Remove the lobsters and place in the platter with prawns. If the skillet is too dry, add more oil. Lower the heat to medium, fold in the pepper, onions and garlic and allow to cook for 12 minutes until soft.
4. Fold in the rice into the skillet and mix with the vegetables.
5. Pour the broth into skillet and allow the mixture to boil, then reduce the heat and allow to simmer for 12 minutes.
6. Lay the prawns, clams, lobster and fish on the surface of the rice, cover with aluminum foil and allow to cook for 12 minutes.
7. Take out the foil cover and cook for further 6 minutes. The rice should be cooked through and the clams should open up.
8. Remove from heat, cover once again with the foil and leave for 16 minutes. Sprinkle parsley on top before serving.
9. Enjoy.

GOLDEN Paella

Prep Time: 15 mins
Total Time: 1 hr 15 mins

Servings per Recipe: 6
Calories   1014.5
Fat   61.5g
Cholesterol   310.1mg
Sodium   943.1mg
Carbohydrates   71.4g
Protein   42.4g

Ingredients

Aioli
2 large egg yolks
1 garlic clove, minced
1 pinch saffron thread
kosher salt
1 C. olive oil
3 tbsp. olive oil
1 tsp. lemon juice
Paella
5 tbsp. extra virgin olive oil
2 onions, diced
5 large plum tomatoes, halved
2 red bell peppers, cored and diced
3 bay leaves
1 tsp. paprika
4 C. fish stock
2 C. short-grain rice
1 C. peas
12 ounces squid rings
1 1/2 lbs. mussels
12 ounces large shrimp, peeled with tails intact
2 tbsp. fresh parsley, chopped
lemon wedge

Directions

1. Whisk the egg yolks, saffron, garlic and a dash of salt with the use of a mixer with the whisk attachment; add olive oil drop by drop.
2. Once the aioli becomes thick in consistency increase the flow of oil into a thin stream; add a bit of lemon juice and more salt if required.
3. Pour olive oil into a skillet with lid and heat well; toss in the onion and temper for 16 minutes until soft.
4. In the meantime, grate the plum tomatoes, slice the edges until the skins are left and dispose the skins.
5. Fold in the tomatoes, bay leaves and peppers to the onions; adjust seasonings with paprika.
6. Allow the mixture to simmer, stir once in a while for about 16 minutes.
7. Pour the stock and allow the mixture to boil. Fold in the rice, lower the heat and allow to simmer for 12 minutes preventing the rice getting stuck to the bottom of the skillet.
8. Add the peas, mussels or clams, squid and shrimp; reduce the heat and allow to simmer for 12 minutes until the liquid becomes fully absorbed.
9. Cover the skillet with lid, transfer from heat and allow to rest for 12 minutes; sprinkle parsley on top and allow the mixture to cool.
10. Serve garnished with wedges of lemon and saffron aioli.
11. Enjoy.

Riverside Paella

Prep Time: 1 hr
Total Time: 1 hr 55 mins

Servings per Recipe: 6	
Calories	873.9
Fat	38.9g
Cholesterol	83.9mg
Sodium	1021.5mg
Carbohydrates	88.7g
Protein	34.4g

Ingredients

- 5 C. chicken broth
- 1/4 tsp. saffron thread
- 1 1/2 lbs. loin lamb, trimmed fat
- 1/2 tsp. salt
- 1/2 tsp. ground black pepper
- 3 tbsp. olive oil
- 6 ounces thick-cut pancetta, diced
- 1 large leek, halved lengthwise then sliced
- 8 baby artichokes, halved, outer leaves removed, stems trimmed
- 1 C. dry light white wine
- 2 tbsp. chopped rosemary
- 2 1/2 C. Arborio rice
- 1 1/2 C. shelled peas

Directions

1. Place the saffron and broth in a pot and heat well. Reduce the heat, cover with lid and maintain the warmth.
2. Place the oven rack in the middle of the oven and before you do anything set the oven to 375F. Rub salt and pepper on lamb loin.
3. Pour olive oil into a skillet and sauté the loin for 7 minutes until a slight brown on all sides; remove the loin to a platter and leave aside.
4. Stir in the pancetta to the skillet, stir often and leave for 5 minutes until a slight brown in color.
5. Toss in the leeks and leave for 4 minutes until soft.
6. Add the baby artichoke halves and leave for 2 minutes until fragrant.
7. Stir in the rosemary and wine; allow the mixture to simmer ensuring to scrape up any food pieces stuck to the bottom of the pan.
8. Leave for 6 minutes until the sauce becomes thick in consistency; stir the mixture occasionally.
9. Fold in the rice and leave for 2 minutes allowing the rice to coat evenly with the sauce.
10. Stir in the warm broth mix and allow to simmer.
11. Lower the heat, uncover and allow to simmer for 12 minutes stirring once in a while.
12. Cut the lamb into 1" parts.
13. Once the rice has cooked in 12 minutes, fold in the lamb parts into the bubbling sauce. Sprinkle peas on top.
14. Place in the preheated oven and leave for about 16 minutes until the liquid becomes dry and the rice is soft and tender.
15. Take out from the oven, place on a wire rack, cover with the use of a foil, and leave for 12 minutes to come to room temperature prior to serving.
16. Enjoy.

SOUTHWEST
Paella

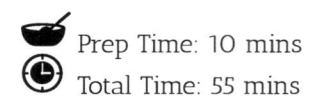

🍳 Prep Time: 10 mins
⏱ Total Time: 55 mins

Servings per Recipe: 6
Calories 576.0
Fat 21.0g
Cholesterol 149.2mg
Sodium 691.5mg
Carbohydrates 58.9g
Protein 39.1g

Ingredients

1/2 lb. frozen shrimp
1/2 lb. frozen clam
1/2 lb. frozen pollock
1/2 lb. frozen octopus
2 tbsp. clarified butter
1 (6 ounce) cans chipotle chilies in adobo
2 tbsp. bouquet garni
2 tbsp. garlic
2 C. saffron rice mix

1 bay leaf
1 large Vidalia onion
6 C. water
1 (12 ounce) cans black beans
6 tortillas, deep fried
2 avocados, wedges
2 limes wedges

Directions

1. Place the clarified butter in a saucepan and allow to melt.
2. Sauté the onions and leave until nearly caramelized.
3. Toss in bouquet garni and bay leaf.
4. Pour water over the ingredients and combine well.
5. Stir in the seafood mix and allow the mixture to boil for 8 minutes.
6. Lower the heat and allow the mixture to simmer. Toss in garlic chipotles in Adobo, garlic or sundried tomato mixture, cover with lid and cook for 48 minutes.
7. Take away the bay leaf and serve into bowls. Serve garnished with lime and avocado.
8. Enjoy.

Paella Calamari

Prep Time: 5 mins
Total Time: 15 mins

Servings per Recipe: 2
Calories   891.2
Fat   36.4g
Cholesterol   93.3mg
Sodium   606.0mg
Carbohydrates   88.3g
Protein   41.2g

Ingredients

1/4 C. olive oil
1 C. uncooked rice
1 C. chicken broth
2 ounces white wine
salt
4 shrimp, deveined
4 scallops
4 clams, scrubbed
4 mussels, scrubbed

2 small lobster tails
1 chicken breast, cubed
parsley
1 tsp. garlic
1/2 C. cooked peas
4 pieces calamari

Directions

1. Prepare the rice according to the package instructions. Once the rice is cooked combine with the peas.
2. Pour oil into a skillet and heat well. Temper the garlic and fold in chicken. Leave for a few minutes and stir in the shellfish.
3. Combine the ingredients with wine, salt and pepper.
4. Serve with cooked rice and sprinkle parsley on top.
5. Enjoy.

HONEY
Saffron Paella

🥣 Prep Time: 20 mins
⏱ Total Time: 30 mins

Servings per Recipe: 6
Calories 529.9
Fat 30.2g
Cholesterol 66.5mg
Sodium 1459.3mg
Carbohydrates 37.7g
Protein 25.0g

Ingredients

- 1 lb. chorizo sausage, removed from casings
- 1/2 C. onion, diced
- 2 garlic cloves, chopped
- 1 C. pumpkin, cooked
- 1/2 C. frozen peas
- 1/2 tsp. cinnamon
- 1/2 tsp. ground nutmeg
- 1/8 tsp. ground cloves
- parsley
- snipped chives
- Rice
- 2 medium tomatoes, chopped
- 1 tbsp. honey
- drizzle olive oil
- salt and pepper
- 4 C. chicken broth
- 1 pinch saffron thread
- 1 C. Arborio rice

Directions

1. Before you do anything set the oven to 325F. To roast the tomatoes, combine the tomatoes, olive oil, honey, salt and pepper. Place the mixture on a slightly buttered parchment sheet. Leave in the oven for 22 minutes.
2. Pour the chicken broth into a saucepan and allow the mixture to boil. Stir in Arborio rice and saffron. Reduce the heat and allow the mixture to simmer for about 22 minutes. Ensure not to drain the rice prior to adding to the paella.
3. Place onion, sausage and garlic in a non-stick pan and heat well. Break the sausage into lumps with the use of a wooden spatula.
4. Allow the mixture to brown and fold in the saffron rice, pumpkin, roasted tomatoes, spices and peas.
5. Allow the mixture to simmer for 12 minutes until thick in consistency. Garnish with chives and fresh parsley and serve warm. Enjoy.

Sweet Mexicana Paella

Prep Time: 20 mins
Total Time: 55 mins

Servings per Recipe: 4
Calories	306.0
Fat	4.5g
Cholesterol	0.0mg
Sodium	165.9mg
Carbohydrates	61.8g
Protein	7.0g

Ingredients

- 1 tbsp. vegetable oil
- 1 onion, chopped
- 2 garlic cloves, minced
- 1 C. short-grain rice
- 1/4 tsp. turmeric
- 2 C. vegetable stock, warm
- 1/4 tsp. salt
- 1/4 tsp. pepper
- 1 sweet red pepper
- 1 sweet green pepper
- 2 plum tomatoes
- 1 1/2 C. corn kernels
- 1 bunch parsley, chopped, leaves only

Directions

1. Pour oil into a pan and heat well; sauté the onion, rice, garlic and turmeric for 5 minutes until the onion becomes soft.
2. Add stock, salt and pepper; allow the mixture to boil; lower the heat, cover with lid and allow to simmer for 12 minutes.
3. In the meantime, slice peppers in half along the length; take out membranes and core; slice in half crosswise and slice into strips.
4. Core and dice the tomatoes.
5. Add the tomatoes and peppers into the pan; cover and cook for 16 minutes until the rice becomes tender.
6. Fold in the corn; cover with lid and cook for 6 minutes until the liquid becomes fully absorbed.
7. Sprinkle parsley on top.
8. Can be served with a crunchy crisp marinated salad and crusty roll.
9. Enjoy.

ROASTED
Paella

Prep Time: 1 hr
Total Time: 1 hr 50 mins

Servings per Recipe: 8
Calories 549.7
Fat 15.3g
Cholesterol 137.6mg
Sodium 1011.7mg
Carbohydrates 59.4g
Protein 40.3g

Ingredients

3 tbsp. olive oil
2 medium onions, chopped
1 red bell pepper, seeded and diced
1/4 lb. Spanish chorizo, sliced and diced
2 garlic cloves, minced
1 tbsp. tomato paste
1 1/4 tsps. smoked paprika
salt
ground black pepper
1 lb. medium grain rice
1 C. clam juice
6 C. fish stock
1 tsp. saffron thread
1 lb. mussels, well-scrubbed
1 lb. jumbo shrimp, peeled and deveined
1 lb. cooked chicken, sliced
1 1/2 C. frozen baby peas
2 tbsp. chopped parsley

Directions

1. Before you do anything set the oven to 350F.
2. Pour the olive oil into a skillet and heat well.
3. Add the onions and sauté for 8 minutes until soft.
4. Toss in the bell pepper and leave for 3 minutes until soft.
5. Stir in the chorizo and sauté for 3 minutes until the sausage is evenly coated with the oil.
6. Fold in the garlic and cook for 35 seconds.
7. Stir in the paprika and tomato paste and leave for about 2 minutes until the mixture slightly darkens in color.
8. Adjust seasonings with salt and pepper.
9. Fold in the rice and cook for 2 minutes. Ensure to stir the rice without browning.
10. Pour in the 1 C. of broth and clam juice into the skillet. Move the skillet using pot holders to ensure that the ingredients are evenly spread out and combined together.
11. Allow to cook for 6 minutes until the liquid is fully absorbed.
12. Stir in the balance broth and the saffron and allow the mixture to boil.
13. Cover with lid and place in the oven.
14. Bake for 38 minutes until the liquid evaporates fully.
15. Transfer the skillet from the oven and fold in the shellfish, peas and sausage and combine well.
16. Cover and place once again in the oven and cook for 16 minutes until the shrimp becomes pink and mussels open up.
17. Take out from the oven and serve.
18. Enjoy.

Chicken and Chorizo Paella

Prep Time: 20 mins
Total Time: 1 hr 20 mins

Servings per Recipe: 8
Calories   275.6
Fat   14.3g
Cholesterol   95.9mg
Sodium   909.7mg
Carbohydrates   8.9g
Protein   26.6g

Ingredients

1 tbsp. olive oil
1/2 lb. boneless skinless chicken breast, cubed
1/2 lb. chorizo sausage, sliced
1 large onion, chopped
1 garlic clove, chopped
1 (10 ounce) packages saffron rice mix (yellow rice)
3 C. water
1 (14 1/2 ounce) cans diced tomatoes
1/2 lb. raw shrimp, peeled and deveined
1 lb. clam, with shells
1 C. frozen peas

Directions

1. Pour the olive oil into a pan and heat well.
2. Toss in the chicken pieces and sauté until a slight brown in color.
3. Take out the chicken from the pan and leave aside.
4. Lower the heat and fold in the slices of sausage and stir fry until nicely browned.
5. Stir in the onion and garlic and leave to cook for 6 minutes until soft; fold in the rice mix, tomatoes and water.
6. Allow the mixture to boil, uncover and leave to simmer for about 22 minutes until the rice becomes tender and the liquid is fully absorbed.
7. Fold in the shrimp, chicken and clams and leave for 12 minutes until the clams open up.
8. Sprinkle peas on top and serve.
9. Enjoy.

PAELLA
Estrellita

Prep Time: 10 mins
Total Time: 40 mins

Servings per Recipe: 4
Calories 324.8
Fat 7.3g
Cholesterol 40.3mg
Sodium 440.2mg
Carbohydrates 47.2g
Protein 15.9g

Ingredients

1 lb. chorizo sausage, removed from casings
1/2 C. onion, diced
2 garlic cloves, chopped
1 C. pumpkin, cooked
1/2 C. frozen peas
1/2 tsp. cinnamon
1/2 tsp. ground nutmeg
1/8 tsp. ground cloves
parsley

snipped chives
Rice
2 medium tomatoes, chopped
1 tbsp. honey
drizzle olive oil
salt and pepper
4 C. chicken broth
1 pinch saffron thread
1 C. Arborio rice

Directions

1. Add the saffron to the broth and allow the mixture to boil. Add tomato, turmeric, paprika, salt and pepper. Heat oil in a skillet.
2. Sauté onion and garlic until tender, then remove from the skillet.
3. Fold in the chicken and allow to brown, and add oil as necessary, then remove from the skillet. Scrape the bottom of the skillet, pour in more oil, fold in rice and cook until tender.
4. Pour the boiling broth and without stirring cook on a medium flame for 6 minutes.
5. Lower the heat, spread the chicken, mussels, red pepper, chorizo and any other optional ingredients and cook for 16 minutes.
6. Cover with lid and cook on a low heat for 6 more minutes. Move the skillet around to keep the heat even.
7. Allow to stand for 6 minutes, ensuring to dispose shellfish that do not open up.
8. Enjoy.

Paella Winters

Prep Time: 20 mins
Total Time: 3 hr 20 mins

Servings per Recipe: 10
Calories	1117.2
Fat	47.5g
Cholesterol	202.8mg
Sodium	879.9mg
Carbohydrates	116.7g
Protein	58.0g

Ingredients

- 1 C. olive oil
- 2 -3 heads garlic
- 6 red peppers, cored, seeded and sliced
- 5 -6 lbs. chicken
- 4 yellow onions, chopped
- 2 (16 ounce) cans diced tomatoes
- 6 -7 1/2 C. chicken stock
- 20 -25 saffron threads, crushed
- 2 -2 1/2 tsps. smoked paprika
- 4 -5 C. short-grain rice
- 2 (16 ounce) cans garbanzo beans
- 1 lb. green beans
- 20 -24 jumbo shrimp
- 20 -24 clams
- 4 -5 lemons wedges

Directions

1. Pour olive oil into a skillet and heat well. Sauté garlic and peppers in the heated oil. Transfer the peppers from the skillet to a dish and leave aside. Toss in the chicken and leave to sear on all sides until golden brown in color. Stir in the onions and cook until soft.
2. Fold in the tomatoes and the stock and leave for 30 minutes.
3. In the meantime, use a mortar and pestle and pound the smoked paprika and saffron and mix it with the stock.
4. After completion of 30 minutes add the rice and allow to simmer for 22 minutes.
5. Ensure not to cover or stir the rice; when the rice is being cooked toss in the garbanzo beans and the vegetables.
6. Add the shellfish and the shrimp into the rice during the last 10 minutes. Finally add the wedges of lemon onto the rim of the skillet.
7. Serve warm. Enjoy.

PAELLA
Summers

Prep Time: 20 mins
Total Time: 1 hr 20 mins

Servings per Recipe: 6
Calories 750.7
Fat 32.5g
Cholesterol 126.8mg
Sodium 976.6mg
Carbohydrates 73.9g
Protein 38.0g

Ingredients

11 ounces raw shrimp, shells on
2 1/4 lbs. mussels
3/4 C. olive oil
1 small onion, chopped
1 garlic clove, chopped
1 large tomatoes, chopped
2 small squid, cleaned and cut into rings
1 lb. long-grain rice
sea salt
3 sprigs fresh parsley
1 pinch saffron thread
2 chicken stock cubes
4 ounces frozen peas
1 red pepper, deseeded and cut into strips
lemon, wedges

Directions

1. Remove the skin and the tails from the shrimp and leave aside. Place the shells and heads in a saucepan of water and allow to simmer for 12 minutes. Transfer from heat and with the use of a colander strain the liquid into a dish.
2. Take out the beards from the mussels and rinse under tap of running water.
3. Dispose shellfish with damaged shells or which don't close when properly tapped.
4. Place the shellfish in a skillet, stir in 1/4 C. of water, cover with lid and cook for 7 minutes until the shells open up.
5. Remove with a spatula and dispose any shellfish that remain closed up. Keep aside the cooking liquid.
6. Remove the shells from the mussels, keeping aside a few shells for garnishing. Add the cooking liquid to the shrimp stock.
7. 7 C. are required and add water as necessary. Fold in the stock into a pot and heat well without boiling.

8. Set the oven to 350F and pour oil into the skillet.
9. Toss in the onion and garlic and cook for 8 minutes until a slight brown in color.
10. Stir in the tomato and leave for a few minutes.
11. Keep a side a little shrimp for garnishing and stir in the balance to the skillet with rice.
12. Allow to cook until the squid is no longer pink. Stir in the mussels and adjust seasonings with salt and add the stock.
13. Toss the skillet gently ensuring to distribute the liquid evenly.
14. Batch the parsley and saffron together; add 2 tbsp water and stir into the skillet. Break the stock cubes into the skillet and combine well.
15. Stir in the peas and leave for a few minutes.
16. Serve garnished with red pepper, kept aside mussels and shrimps. Place in the oven and cook for 30 minutes.
17. Decorate the rim of the skillet with wedges of lemon.
18. Enjoy.

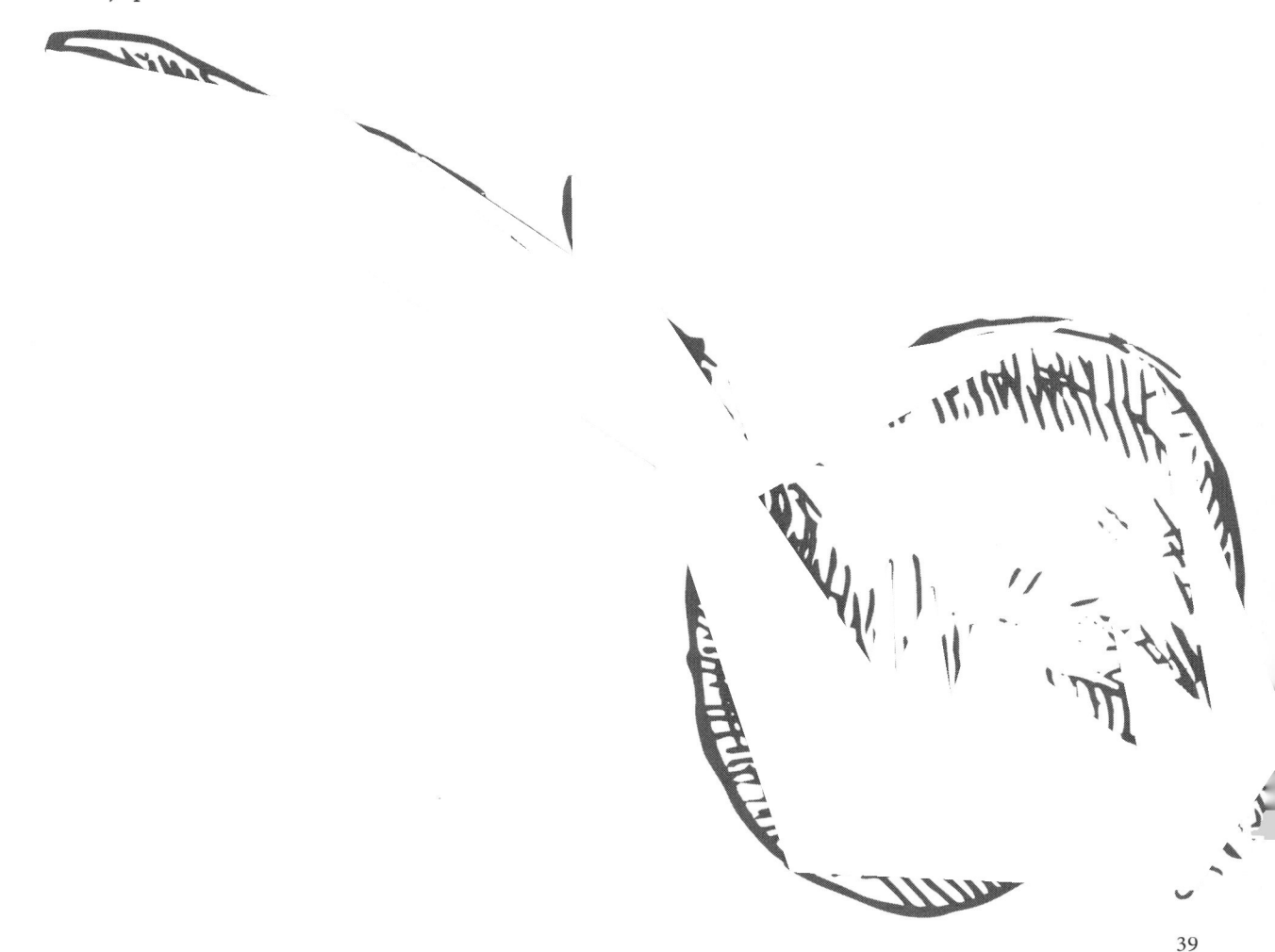

WHITE and Brown Rice Paella

Prep Time: 5 mins
Total Time: 30 mins

Servings per Recipe: 2
Calories   784.3
Fat   40.6g
Cholesterol   119.0mg
Sodium   819.0mg
Carbohydrates   70.1g
Protein   35.8g

Ingredients

1/4 C. long grain white rice
1/4 C. long grain brown rice
1/2 C. coconut milk
1/4 C. water
3 tbsp. crushed pineapple
8 andouille sausages, slices
1/4 lb. chorizo sausage
8 white pearl onions
1/4 lb. catfish, cut into pieces
8 large shrimp

Directions

1. Pour coconut milk and water into a pan and add rice. Allow the mixture to boil, lower the heat and allow to simmer for 12 minutes.
2. Stir in the balance ingredients excluding shrimp and cook for further 12 minutes; stir often.
3. At this point the rice should be half cooked and there should be some liquid left in the pan. Add more water if required.
4. Toss in the shrimp and allow to cook until they are pink in color.
5. If the mixture is moist, take out the shrimp and continue to cook until the liquid is fully absorbed. Add the shrimp once again and serve.
6. Enjoy..

Portuguese Pan

Prep Time: 45 mins
Total Time: 1 hr 40 mins

Servings per Recipe: 6
Calories	465.5
Fat	19.7g
Cholesterol	219.1mg
Sodium	1142.8mg
Carbohydrates	38.5g
Protein	31.7g

Ingredients

- 1/2 lb. chorizo sausage
- 1 small red bell pepper, chopped
- 1 small yellow bell pepper, chopped
- 1 onion, chopped
- 2 garlic cloves, minced
- 1/4 tsp. crushed saffron thread
- 1 lb. shrimp, peeled, deveined, and chopped
- 1 (3 1/2 ounce) cans smoked mussels, drained
- 2 C. cooked white rice
- 1 C. Italian seasoned breadcrumbs
- 1/2 C. chopped flat leaf parsley
- 1/4 C. green olives, sliced
- 2 tbsp. lemon juice
- 1/2 tsp. ground cumin
- 1/2 tsp. cayenne pepper
- 1/4 tsp. salt
- 2 eggs

Directions

1. Before you do anything set the oven to 350F; remove the sausage from its cover and break the meat into a non-stick pan.
2. Cook the sausage, stir once in a while and allow to cook for 6 minutes until a slight brown in color.
3. Drain the excess grease; stir in the onions and peppers into the pan.
4. Lower the heat, stir once in a while and leave for 6 minutes until the vegetables are soft.
5. Fold in the saffron and garlic, stir and allow to cook for 2 minutes.
6. Place the shrimp, rice, mussels, parsley, bread crumbs, lemon juice, olive, cayenne, cumin, eggs, salt and cooked vegetable/sausage mixture in a bowl and combine well with the use of your hands.
7. Fold in the mixture to a loaf pan; bake for 50 minutes until the top is crusty and the loaf becomes brown in color.
8. Allow the loaf to stand in the loaf pan for 12 minutes. Slice into squares and serve.
9. Enjoy.

OUR
Best Paella

Prep Time: 25 mins
Total Time: 1 hr 25 mins

Servings per Recipe: 10
Calories 347.3
Fat 9.0g
Cholesterol 151.4mg
Sodium 1257.6mg
Carbohydrates 38.4g
Protein 26.4g

Ingredients

8 ounces sausage, cut into pieces
15 raw chicken strips
2 lbs. large shrimp
1 onion, chopped
1 green bell pepper
1 stalk celery, chopped
2 garlic cloves, minced
2 C. uncooked long grain rice

2 (14 1/2 ounce) cans diced tomatoes
2 bay leaves
2 tsps. salt
1 tsp. dried oregano
3/4 tsp. ground turmeric
3 1/2 C. chicken broth

Directions

1. Heat a skillet and sauté sausage pieces until nicely browned on all sides. Transfer the sausage into a platter, and sauté the chicken in the sausage fat until nicely browned.
2. Transfer the chicken into the platter. Stir fry the onions, celery, green pepper and garlic for 6 minutes until soft.
3. Fold in the rice, bay leaves, tomatoes, turmeric, oregano and salt, combine well and cook for 2 minutes. Fold in the chicken broth and the kept aside tomato juice into the mixture.
4. Stir in the chicken, cover with lid and allow to simmer for 22 minutes.
5. Toss in the sausages and allow to simmer for 16 minutes; add the shrimp, cover with lid and cook for 12 minutes until the shrimp becomes pink in color.
6. Enjoy.

Paella Zaragoza

Prep Time: 15 mins
Total Time: 40 mins

Servings per Recipe: 8
Calories 629.4
Fat 26.0g
Cholesterol 173.6mg
Sodium 1447.3mg
Carbohydrates 47.7g
Protein 47.5g

Ingredients

3 tbsp. extra virgin olive oil
3 garlic cloves, crushed
1/2 tsp. crushed red pepper flakes
2 C. enriched white rice
1/4 tsp. saffron thread
1 bay leaf
1 quart chicken broth
4 spring thyme
1 1/2 lbs. chicken tenders, cut into thirds
salt
ground pepper
1 red bell pepper, seeded and chopped
Toppings
1 medium onion, chopped
3/4 lb. chorizo sausage, casing removed and sliced
1 lb. large shrimp, peeled and deveined
18 green lipped mussels, cleaned
1 C. frozen peas
2 lemons, zested
1/4 C. flat leaf parsley, chopped
4 scallions, chopped
lemon wedge
crusty bread

Directions

1. Pour 2 tbsp extra virgin olive oil into a skillet and heat well. Add the garlic, rice and red pepper flakes and sauté for 4 minutes
2. Fold in saffron threads, broth, bay leaf and thyme and allow the mixture to boil. Cover with lid and allow the mixture to simmer.
3. Add 1 tbsp of extra virgin olive oil into another skillet and brown the chicken on all sides. Sprinkle salt and pepper on the chicken.
4. Toss in onions and peppers to the skillet and leave for 4 minutes. Fold in the chorizo to the skillet and cook for further 3 minutes. Take out the skillet from heat.
5. After about 15 minutes, stir in the shellfish to the rice. Sprinkle peas and lemon zest over the rice mixture, then cover with lid. After 6 minutes remove the lid and dispose any mussel shells which do not open up.
6. Fold in the rice and seafood mix and discard the bay and thyme leaves. Spread the chicken, onions, peppers and chorizo in the skillet.
7. Sprinkle parsley and scallions on top.
8. Serve garnished with lemon wedges and warm crusty bread.
9. Enjoy.

POLISH
Paella

Prep Time: 20 mins
Total Time: 45 mins

Servings per Recipe: 6
Calories   635.0
Fat   26.8g
Cholesterol   101.9mg
Sodium   960.0mg
Carbohydrates   61.3g
Protein   34.0g

Ingredients

1 lb. boneless skinless chicken, cubed
1 lb. kielbasa, cubed
1 medium onion, diced
1 tbsp. bottled garlic
1 tomatoes, diced
1 bell pepper, diced
1/2 C. frozen peas
3 C. chicken stock

2 C. long-grain rice
1 tbsp. olive oil
1 tsp. turmeric
1 bay leaf
salt & pepper

Directions

1. Before you do anything set the oven to 350F.
2. Rub salt and pepper on the chicken.
3. Pour oil into a pan with lid and heat well; pan fry the chicken until a nice brown in color.
4. Transfer the chicken from the pan.
5. Place the pan once again on the heat and fold in onion, kielbasa and bell pepper.
6. Pan fry until the kielbasa turns brown and the onions become soft.
7. Fold in the tomato and transfer the chicken back again into the pan.
8. Add the rice, chicken stock, bay leaf and the turmeric.
9. Allow the mixture to boil.
10. Place the peas on top.
11. Cover the pan with lid and set in the oven.
12. Bake for 27 minutes until the rice is cooked and the liquid is absorbed.
13. Enjoy.

City Park Paella

Prep Time:	10 mins
Total Time:	40 mins

Servings per Recipe: 4
Calories 559.0
Fat 18.9g
Cholesterol 161.5mg
Sodium 1166.4mg
Carbohydrates 62.0g
Protein 37.4g

Ingredients

1 tbsp. olive oil
1/2 C. onion, chopped
6 ounces chicken sausage, cooked and sliced
2 (3 1/2 ounce) packages brown rice
salt
1/2 tsp. smoked paprika
1/4 tsp. black pepper

1 (15 ounce) cans chicken broth
1 (14 1/2 ounce) cans diced tomatoes, undrained
2 tsps. garlic, minced
1 1/2 C. edamame, frozen. shelled
1/4 tsp. saffron thread
1/2 lb. frozen shrimp, thawed

Directions

1. Pour oil into a skillet and heat well. Toss in onions and sausage and pan fry until the onions become soft.
2. Fold in the rice to the skillet.
3. Stir frequently and add the paprika, salt and pepper and fry for 32 seconds.
4. Fold in tomatoes, chicken broth and garlic and allow the mixture to boil.
5. Cover with lid and allow to simmer for 12 minutes until the liquid is fully absorbed and rice is cooked.
6. Add the saffron and edamame.
7. Fold in the shrimp to the rice mix, cover with lid and cook for 5 minutes until the liquid is fully absorbed.
8. Enjoy.

NEW ENGLAND
Paella

🥣 Prep Time: 20 mins
🕐 Total Time: 1 hr 35 mins

Servings per Recipe: 4
Calories   598.9
Fat   15.1g
Cholesterol   87.2mg
Sodium   832.8mg
Carbohydrates   75.8g
Protein   27.7g

Ingredients

4 lobster tails
8 stone crab claws
12 large shrimp
8 large clams, washed and scrubbed
8 large mussels, washed and scrubbed
2 green peppers, seeded and chopped
4 -5 plum tomatoes, peeled and chopped
2 cloves garlic, peeled and minced
1/8 tsp. red pepper flakes
salt and pepper
1 pinch saffron
1 1/2 C. long grain rice, rinsed
1/4 C. unsalted butter, softened
3 C. chicken broth
1 C. dry white wine
1 (10 ounce) boxes frozen green peas
roasted red pepper, strips

Directions

1. Before you do anything set the oven to 400F.
2. Pour salted water into a saucepan and heat mussels, clams and shrimp and leave for 4 minutes; transfer from water and leave aside.
3. Throw away any clams or mussels which do not open up.
4. Baste butter on lobster tails.
5. Cover crab claws and lobster tails with aluminum foil and leave in the oven for 16 minutes.
6. Sauté onions, green peppers, garlic and tomatoes in a skillet until garlic become soft.
7. Stir in red pepper flakes, saffron, salt and pepper.
8. Fold in the rice and pan fry for 4 minutes.
9. Add the wine and the broth and allow the mixture to simmer for 22 minutes.
10. Toss in the peas.
11. Cover with lid and allow to cook for 16 minutes.
12. Stir once in a while to ensure the liquid is fully absorbed by the rice.
13. Lay the lobster, shrimp, clams, stone crab and mussels on top.
14. Cover with lid and heat for further 12 minutes.
15. Transfer the mixture to a dish.
16. Serve garnished with roasted red peppers.
17. Enjoy.

Sun Dried Parmesan Paella

Prep Time: 20 mins
Total Time: 50 mins

Servings per Recipe: 6
Calories 443.2
Fat 14.6g
Cholesterol 73.6mg
Sodium 561.8mg
Carbohydrates 43.3g
Protein 32.1g

Ingredients

1 tbsp. oil
1 1/2 C. rice
3 C. chicken broth, rich
1 tsp. turmeric
1/2 tsp. cumin, ground
salt and pepper
1 garlic clove, minced
4 shallots, minced

3 sun-dried tomatoes, drained and chopped
1/4 C. chicken broth
4 C. cooked chicken, diced
1/4 C. pine nuts, toasted
1/4 C. parmesan cheese

Directions

1. Place the first six ingredients in a skillet and leave for 32 minutes until the liquid is fully absorbed and the rice becomes tender.
2. In the meantime, place the next four ingredients in a saucepan and allow to cook until the shallots are tender.
3. Fold in the chicken and allow to heat through.
4. Fold in the tomato mixture into the rice and combine well.
5. Place the mixture in a platter and sprinkle pine nuts and cheese on top.
6. Enjoy.

SOUTHERN
Barcelona Paella

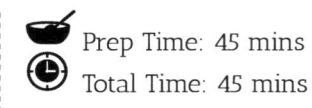

Prep Time: 45 mins
Total Time: 45 mins

Servings per Recipe: 6
Calories 869.1
Fat 36.9g
Cholesterol 121.6mg
Sodium 1320.6mg
Carbohydrates 82.8g
Protein 47.6g

Ingredients

10 medium chicken drumsticks
1/2 C. extra virgin olive oil
2 C. medium shrimp
1 medium Spanish onion, diced
1/2 C. pureed ripe tomatoes
1 tsp. kosher salt
1 tsp. saffron thread
2 tbsp. sweet pimientos
4 quarts chicken stock
2 C. bomba
1 lb. manila clams, scrubbed
1 C. fresh peas
10 asparagus spears, sliced
1 inch piece sausage

Directions

1. Before you do anything set the oven to 400F. Spread the chicken drumsticks on a parchment sheet and season with olive oil and salt. Leave in the oven for 25 minutes and leave aside.
2. Meanwhile, heat a skillet, pour the oil and leave until smoking. Toss in the shrimp and allow to cook until brown in color on all sides, on 4 minutes on each side.
3. Remove to a dish and leave aside. Toss in the onion and cook for 9 minutes until soft. Move the onions into the middle of the pan and add 2 tbsp of salt to the sides of the pan.
4. Stir in the tomato puree and cook for 4 minutes. Sprinkle the balance salt, pimenton and saffron and cook for 6 minutes.
5. Pour chicken stock and allow the mixture to boil for 6 minutes. Fold in the rice and combine well. Stir in clams and drumsticks and arrange them in the pan.
6. Fold in the asparagus and peas and allow the mixture to boil ensuring not to stir, for 12 minutes. Adjust seasonings as required and allow to cook for further 10 minutes until the liquid has evaporated.
7. Transfer from the heat and allow to rest for 12 minutes prior to serving.
8. Enjoy.

Weekend Paella

Prep Time: 30 mins
Total Time: 2 hrs

Servings per Recipe: 6
Calories	271.4
Fat	9.6g
Cholesterol	8.8mg
Sodium	306.3mg
Carbohydrates	36.9g
Protein	8.6g

Ingredients

- 2 tbsp. vegetable oil
- 1 onion, sliced
- 1 red pepper, cored, seeded and sliced
- 1 garlic clove, crushed
- 1 C. long grain rice
- 1 quart chicken stock
- 1 tsp. paprika
- 1 tsp. turmeric
- 1 C. frozen peas
- 3/4 C. smoked ham, ends diced
- 1/4 C. bacon, ends diced

Directions

1. Pour oil into a skillet and heat well. Sauté the onion for 5 minutes until soft. Fold in the bacon and cook until a slight golden in color.
2. Stir in the red pepper, rice and garlic and pan fry for 2 minutes.
3. Fold in the ham, paprika, stock and turmeric and allow the mixture to boil and then simmer for 15 minutes.
4. Combine the mixture with peas and bacon bits and cook for 5 more minutes until the rice and vegetables are soft and tender.
5. Adjust seasonings and serve warm.
6. Enjoy.

CLASSICAL
One-Pot Hot Pot

🍲 Prep Time: 20 mins
🕐 Total Time: 55 mins

Servings per Recipe: 6
Calories   284.3
Cholesterol   81.0mg
Sodium   542.4mg
Carbohydrates   34.1g
Protein   20.7g

Ingredients

1 tbsp olive oil
1/2 lb chunk chicken
1 C. rice, uncooked
1 medium chopped onion
2 tsp garlic, minced
1 1/2 C. chicken broth
1 (8 oz.) cans stewed tomatoes, chopped reserving liquid
1/2-1 tsp paprika

1/8-1/4 tsp ground red pepper
1/8-1/4 tsp saffron
1/2 lb medium shrimp, peeled and deveined
1 small red pepper, cut into strips
1 small green pepper, cut into strips
1/2 C. frozen green pea

Directions

1. In a Dutch oven, heat the oil and stir fry the chicken till golden brown.
2. Stir in the rice, onion and garlic and cook, stirring occasionally till the rice becomes golden brown.
3. Add the broth, tomatoes with liquid, saffron, paprika and red pepper and bring to a boil.
4. Reduce the heat and simmer, covered for about 10 minutes.

Stunning Paella

Prep Time: 5 mins
Total Time: 30 mins

Servings per Recipe: 5
Calories   603.9
Cholesterol   351.8mg
Sodium   850.3mg
Carbohydrates   74.6g
Protein   43.2g

Ingredients

- 1 lb fresh shrimp
- 1 lb squid
- 1 lb mussels
- 2 C. short-grain rice
- 1 onion, minced
- 1 tbsp tomato paste
- 1/2 green pepper
- 1/2 red pepper
- 2 garlic cloves, minced
- 3 tbsp olive oil
- 1/2 tsp saffron thread
- salt
- pepper
- 5 C. water

Directions

1. In a large pan, heat half of the oil and sauté the onion for about 3 minutes.
2. Stir in the bell peppers and tomato paste and sauté for about 2-3 minutes.
3. Stir in rice, squids, saffron, salt and black pepper and sauté for about 2-3 minutes.
4. Add the warm water and the remaining oil and cook till the liquid is absorbed.
5. Add the mussels and shrimp and cook, stirring occasionally for about 10 minutes.

PAELLA
in Mediterranean Style

Prep Time: 20 mins
Total Time: 45 mins

Servings per Recipe: 4
Calories   484.3
Cholesterol   52.5mg
Sodium   1207.2mg
Carbohydrates   51.1g
Protein   26.6g

Ingredients

3 tbsp olive oil
1 medium onion, chopped
2 tbsp fresh minced garlic
1 tsp dried chili pepper flakes
1 small red bell pepper, seeded and chopped
1 C. frozen artichoke heart, thawed
3/4 C. sliced pitted olive
1 (14 oz.) cans chicken broth

1 C. water
1 C. uncooked long-grain white rice
salt, to taste
1/2 tsp paprika
1 pinch saffron thread
black pepper
2 C. cooked chicken, chopped
3/4 C. frozen green pea, thawed

Directions

1. In a large skillet, heat the oil on medium heat and sauté the onion, bell pepper, garlic and chili flakes for about 3 minutes.
2. Stir in the olives and artichokes and sauté for about 2 minutes.
3. Add the water and broth and bring to a boil.
4. Reduce the heat to medium-low and simmer, covered for about 15 minutes.
5. Stir in the chicken and peas and simmer, covered for about 5-7 minutes.
6. Remove everything from the heat and keep aside, covered for about 5 minutes before serving.

Classico
Paella

🥣 Prep Time: 30 mins
🕐 Total Time: 1 hr 30 mins

Servings per Recipe: 5
Calories 787.1
Cholesterol 222.8mg
Sodium 1117.0mg
Carbohydrates 30.8g
Protein 53.5g

Ingredients

- 2 tbsp olive oil, divided.
- 2 1/2-3 lb. chicken, cut into 8 pieces
- 8 oz. chorizo sausages, cut into 1 inch pieces
- 2 cloves garlic, chopped
- 1 medium yellow onion, chopped
- 1 C. uncooked white rice
- 1 tsp saffron
- 2 C. beef broth
- 1 large roasted red pepper, cut into thin strips
- 1/4 C. chopped green onion
- 1/4 C. chopped fresh cilantro
- 1 jalapeno pepper, seeded and chopped
- 1/4 tsp crushed red pepper flakes
- 1/2 lb medium shrimp, shelled and deveined
- 1/2 C. green peas

Directions

1. In a paella pan, heat 1 tbsp of the oil and stir fry the chicken and sausage for about 20 minutes.
2. Transfer the chicken and sausage to a paper towel lined plate and cover with a foil paper to keep warm.
3. Drain off the fat from the pan and wipe it with some paper towel.
4. In the same pan, heat the remaining oil and sauté the onion and garlic for about 5 minutes.
5. Stir in the rice and saffron and stir fry for about 2 minutes.
6. Add the broth and bring to a boil.
7. Reduce the heat to low and simmer, covered for about 30 minutes.
8. Stir in the cooked chicken, sausage and remaining ingredients except the shrimp and peas and simmer, stirring occasionally for about 15 minutes.
9. Stir in the shrimp and peas and simmer for about 5 minutes.

SUMMER
Veggie Paella

Prep Time: 35 mins
Total Time: 1 hr 5 mins

Servings per Recipe: 4
Calories   173.5
Cholesterol   0.0mg
Sodium   169.4mg
Carbohydrates   31.8g
Protein   4.3g

Ingredients

2 tbsp olive oil
1 C. chopped onion
1 C. chopped red pepper
2 tsp finely chopped fresh garlic
1 C. uncooked long grain rice
1 (14 1/2 oz.) can stewed tomatoes
1 (14 1/2 oz.) can vegetable broth
1 C. finely chopped carrot
1 tsp paprika

1 (6 1/2 oz.) jar marinated artichoke hearts, drained
1 C. eggplant, cubed
1 C. zucchini, cubed
1/2 C. frozen peas, thawed
1/4 C. chopped fresh parsley

Directions

1. In a large pan, heat the oil on medium-high heat and sauté the red pepper, onion and garlic for about 2-3 minutes.
2. Stir in the rice and stir fry for about 1 minute.
3. Add the broth, tomatoes, carrots and paprika and bring to a boil.
4. Reduce the heat to medium-low and simmer, covered for about 10 minutes, stirring once half way.
5. Stir in the eggplant, artichokes and zucchini simmer, stirring occasionally for about 10-12 minutes.
6. Stir in the peas and parsley and simmer for about 3-4 minutes.

Paella Forever

Prep Time: 20 mins
Total Time: 50 mins

Servings per Recipe:	6
Calories	398.2
Cholesterol	120.8mg
Sodium	1142.9mg
Carbohydrates	36.8g
Protein	27.7g

Ingredients

- 1 tbsp olive oil
- 3/4 lb large shrimp, peeled and deveined
- 3/4 tsp salt, divided
- 1/4 tsp ground black pepper, divided
- 1/2 C. chorizo sausage, thinly sliced
- 2 boneless skinless chicken thighs, quartered
- 1 C. onion, chopped
- 3 garlic cloves, minced
- 1/2 C. tomatoes, chopped
- 1 tbsp capers, drained
- 1/4 tsp saffron thread, crushed
- 1 C. Arborio rice
- 2/3 C. white wine
- 14 oz. fat-free low-chicken broth
- 1/2 C. frozen green pea
- 1/4 C. water
- 18 mussels
- 2 1/2 tbsp roasted red peppers, chopped
- 2 tbsp cilantro, chopped

Directions

1. In a large pan, heat the oil on medium-high and add the shrimp, salt and black pepper.
2. Stir fry the shrimp for about 4 minutes and transfer it into a bowl.
3. Add the chorizo and cook for about 1 minute and transfer into a bowl.
4. Add the chicken, salt and black pepper and sear for about 2 minutes per side.
5. Add the onion and garlic and stir fry for about 2 minutes.
6. Stir in the tomato, capers and saffron and stir fry for about 1 minute.
7. Add the rice, broth, wine, salt and black pepper and bring to a boil.
8. Reduce the heat and simmer, covered for about 25 minutes.
9. Stir in the shrimp, chorizo, mussels, peas and water and simmer for about 8 minutes.
10. Stir in the bell peppers and cilantro and remove from the heat.
11. Keep aside, covered for about 3 minutes before serving.

GRAND THEFT
Paella

🍳 Prep Time: 15 mins
🕐 Total Time: 55 mins

Servings per Recipe: 6
Calories   440.3
Cholesterol   8.6mg
Sodium   589.4mg
Carbohydrates   52.7g
Protein   10.2g

Ingredients

3 1/4 C. vegetable broth
1 1/2 tbsp chopped parsley
1 tsp dried basil
1/2 tsp saffron
1/4 tsp ground cumin
6 tbsp olive oil
4 tbsp pine nuts
1 large onion, chopped fine
8 garlic cloves, minced

1 medium green bell pepper, chopped fine
3/4 C. pimento stuffed olive, chopped
5 C. spinach leaves, destemmed and chopped
1 1/2 C. rice
1/2 C. parmesan cheese, grated

Directions

1. In a pan, mix together the broth, herbs, saffron and cumin on low heat
2. In a large paella pan, heat the oil and stir fry the pine nuts till lightly toasted.
3. Add the bell pepper, onion and garlic till tender.
4. Add the spinach and olives and cook till the spinach is wilted.
5. Sir in the rice and add the broth mixture and bring to a boil.
6. Reduce the heat and simmer, covered for about 25 minutes.
7. Stir in the cheese and remove from the heat.

Restaurant Style Paella

Prep Time: 20 mins
Total Time: 50 mins

Servings per Recipe: 4
Calories   555.9
Cholesterol   139.4mg
Sodium   860.0mg
Carbohydrates   61.0g
Protein   42.1g

Ingredients

2 tsp sesame oil
125 g shallots
20 g gingerroot
2 garlic cloves
400 g chicken breasts
salt and pepper
250 g orzo pasta
1 1/2 tsp smoked paprika
600 ml chicken stock

225 - 250 g prawns
1/4 C. lemon juice
3 tsp soy sauce
1/3 C. coriander leaves

Directions

1. In a large pan, heat the oil on medium heat and sauté the shallots, garlic and ginger till tender.
2. Add the chicken, salt and black pepper and cook till golden brown.
3. Stir in the orzo and paprika and cook till it just starts to absorb the flavors.
4. Add enough broth to cover the mixture and bring to a boil.
5. Simmer, stirring occasionally for about 15 minutes.
6. Stir in the prawns, soy sauce, lemon juice and seasoning and cook till done.
7. Remove everything from the heat and keep aside, covered for about 3-5 minutes before serving.
8. Stir in the coriander and serve.

SWEDISH
Paella

Prep Time: 30 mins
Total Time: 1 hr 45 mins

Servings per Recipe: 4
Calories   485.6
Cholesterol   128.4mg
Sodium   1451.0mg
Carbohydrates   42.9g
Protein   29.3g

Ingredients

2 tbsp onions, minced
1 tbsp butter
1 C. rice
2 C. water
2 tsp salt
1/2 tsp garlic powder
1/2 tsp black pepper
1 pinch saffron threads
1/4 red pepper, cut into strips

1/4 green pepper, cut into strips
1/4-1/2 lb shrimp, cleaned
1 lb chicken, cut into small pieces
1/2 C. frozen peas
black olives, sliced (to garnish)

Directions

1. Set your oven to 350 degrees F before doing anything else.
2. For the pilaf, in a large pan, melt the butter and stir fry the rice and onion till golden brown.
3. Add the water and salt and bring to a boil.
4. Reduce the heat to low and simmer, covered for about 20 minutes.
5. For the paella, in a baking dish, mix together the cooked pilaf, chicken, bell peppers and spices and cook everything in the oven for 10-20 minutes.
6. Stir in the peas and shrimp and cook for about 5 minutes more.
7. Serve with a garnishing of olives.

Paella for Celebrations

Prep Time: 30 mins
Total Time: 1 hr 30 mins

Servings per Recipe: 8
Calories   639.6
Cholesterol   110.9mg
Sodium   1003.8mg
Carbohydrates   68.9g
Protein   45.1g

Ingredients

- 6 boneless skinless chicken breasts
- 3 chorizo sausage, sliced
- 18 large shrimp, shelled & deveined
- 1 lb mussels
- 2 tbsp olive oil
- 5 C. chicken broth
- 1 C. white wine
- 1 pinch saffron
- 1 onion, chopped
- 3 garlic cloves, chopped
- salt, pepper, paprika
- 1 C. peas
- 1 (4 oz.) jars pimientos
- 3 C. arborio rice

Directions

1. Set your oven to 400 degrees F before doing anything else.
2. In a skillet, heat 1 tbsp of the oil and brown the sausage completely and transfer into a plate.
3. In the same skillet, heat more oil and brown the chicken completely and transfer onto a plate.
4. In the same skillet, heat the remaining oil and sauté the onion and garlic till softened.
5. Add the wine, broth and spices and bring to a boil, stirring continuously.
6. Cook till the liquid reduces slightly.
7. Stir in the sausage, chicken, pimentos and peas and cook in the oven for about 10 minutes.
8. Serve with a garnishing of parsley.

MOUNTAIN-STYLE Paella

Prep Time: 30 mins
Total Time: 1 hr 10 mins

Servings per Recipe: 8
Calories 477.1
Cholesterol 135.0mg
Sodium 1109.0mg
Carbohydrates 49.8g
Protein 31.2g

Ingredients

2 (14 oz.) cans chicken broth
3/4 C. white wine
1/4 C. vermouth, optional
1 tsp turmeric
2 tsp paprika
1 lb boneless skinless chicken thighs, cut into strips
1/2 lb Italian sausage, casing removed and cut into small pieces
1 tbsp olive oil
1 large green bell pepper, cut into thin slices
1 large red bell pepper, cut into thin slices
1 large white onion, halved and sliced thin
2 jalapeno peppers, seeded and chopped
5 cloves garlic, minced
1 tsp thyme
1 tsp oregano
1/2 tsp ground coriander
2 C. rice (short grain works best)
1 lb medium shrimp, raw, shells and tails removed
4 roma tomatoes, chopped
1 1/2 C. fresh green beans, sliced into ½ inch pieces
1/2 C. black olives, sliced

Directions

1. In a pan, mix together the broth, vermouth, wine, paprika and turmeric and bring to a gentle simmer, stirring occasionally.
2. In a large skillet, brown the sausage completely and transfer onto a plate.
3. In the same skillet, brown the chicken strips completely and transfer onto a plate.
4. In the same skillet, heat the oil and sauté the peppers, onion and garlic till tender.
5. Add the spices in the hot broth mixture and stir to combine.
6. In the same skillet, add the broth mixture, chicken and sausage and bring to a boil.
7. Add the rice and gently stir to combine and tuck the shrimp in the rice mixture.

8. Place the tomatoes, beans and olives on top.
9. Bring to a boil and reduce the heat. Cook, covered for about 20 minutes.
10. Remove everything from the heat and keep aside, covered for about 10 minutes before serving.

RICH
Paella

🍳 Prep Time: 15 mins
🕐 Total Time: 1 hr 15 mins

Servings per Recipe: 8
Calories   582.6
Cholesterol   53.5mg
Sodium   1633.1mg
Carbohydrates   50.8g
Protein   27.8g

Ingredients

2 C. quinoa, rinsed well
2 tbsp olive oil
1 lb chorizo sausage, peeled
5 garlic cloves, coarsely chopped
2 red bell peppers, seeded and roughly chopped
1 serrano pepper, minced
1 onion, chopped
2 tsp salt
1/2 tsp black pepper
1 C. frozen lima beans
1 (15 oz.) cans cannellini beans
2 tomatoes, seeded and chopped
4 C. chicken stock
2 tbsp parsley, chopped
2 lemons, cut into wedges

Directions

1. In a bowl, soak the quinoa in cold water for about 15 minutes and drain well.
2. Heat a large pan on medium-high heat and cook the quinoa for about 15 minutes, stirring occasionally.
3. Transfer the quinoa into a bowl.
4. In the same pan, heat the oil and cook the sausage for about 10 minutes, breaking the sausage into little pieces.
5. Stir in the bell peppers, onion, serrano, salt and black pepper and sauté for about 5 minutes.
6. Stir in the tomatoes, both beans and broth and bring to a boil.
7. Reduce the heat to low and simmer for about 15 minutes.
8. Remove everything from the heat and keep aside, covered for about 10 minutes before serving.
9. Serve hot with a garnishing of parsley.

Authentic Seafood Paella in Spanish Style

Prep Time: 1 hr
Total Time: 1 hr 45 mins

Servings per Recipe: 8
Calories   887.3
Cholesterol   344.9mg
Sodium   1820.9mg
Carbohydrates   76.8g
Protein   74.1g

Ingredients

2 1/2 lb. chicken parts
1/4 C. olive oil
1 medium onion, finely diced
4 garlic cloves, minced
2 tsp salt
fresh ground pepper
1/2 tsp paprika
1 large red bell pepper, roasted, peeled, seeded, and diced
1/2 C. sliced green onion
1 lb squid, cleaned, sacs cut into rings
1/2 tsp saffron thread
1 lb large raw shrimp, peeled and deveined
3 C. short-grain rice
6 C. warm chicken stock
1 1/2 lb. small live clams
1 C. frozen peas

Directions

1. Cut each leg of the chicken into 4 pieces and each breast half into 3 pieces.
2. In a paella pan, heat the oil on low heat and sauté the onion and garlic till the onion just starts to sizzle.
3. Increase the heat to medium and cook the chicken pieces with the paprika, salt and black pepper in batches till golden brown.
4. Add the squid, peppers, green onion, salt, black pepper and crumbled saffron.
5. Stir in the rice and stir fry for about 1 minute.
6. Add enough warm broth to cover the mixture and top it with the shrimp and clams.
7. Simmer for about 10 minutes.
8. Top everything with the peas and simmer for about 10 minutes more.

MIDWEEK
Paella

Prep Time: 15 mins
Total Time: 45 mins

Servings per Recipe: 4
Calories   549.8
Cholesterol   110.5mg
Sodium   704.6mg
Carbohydrates   48.5g
Protein   40.5g

Ingredients

1/2 lb hot Italian sausage, cut into 1/2 inch cubes
1 onion, chopped
1 green bell pepper, chopped
2 garlic cloves, minced
1 C. long-grain rice
14 oz. canned tomatoes, chopped
1 C. chicken stock
1/2 tsp ground turmeric

1/4 tsp cayenne pepper
1 lb boneless skinless chicken breast, remove all visible fat and cut into 1 inch cubes
salt and pepper
1 green onion, chopped diagonally

Directions

1. In a large microwave safe dish, mix together the sausage, green pepper, onion and garlic.
2. Microwave on high for about 4-6 minutes, stirring once half way.
3. Add the rice, tomatoes, cayenne pepper, turmeric and broth and stir to combine.
4. Cover the dish and microwave it on high for about 8-10 minutes.
5. Stir everything well, cover the dish and microwave on medium for about 7-9 minutes.
6. Remove everything from the heat and keep it aside, covered for about 5 minutes before serving.
7. Serve hot with a garnishing of green onions.

Distinctive Paella

Prep Time: 20 mins
Total Time: 45 mins

Servings per Recipe: 4
Calories   484.0
Cholesterol   75.6mg
Sodium   1169.7mg
Carbohydrates   57.4g
Protein   26.7g

Ingredients

- 2 tbsp vegetable oil
- 1 onion, sliced
- 1 red pepper, cored, seeded and sliced
- 1 garlic clove, crushed
- 200 g long grain rice
- 180 g smoked ham, roughly diced
- 900 ml chicken stock
- 1/2 tsp paprika
- 1/2 tsp turmeric
- 100 g large shrimp
- 100 g frozen peas
- salt & freshly ground black pepper

Directions

1. In a large pan, heat the oil and sauté the onion for about 3-4 minutes.
2. Add the rice and garlic and stir fry for about 1 minute.
3. Stir in the remaining ingredients except the prawns and peas and bring to a boil.
4. Simmer for about 12 minutes.
5. Stir in the prawns and peas and simmer for about 3-4 minutes.
6. Serve immediately.

MEXICAN
Paella

Prep Time: 10 mins
Total Time: 55 mins

Servings per Recipe: 4
Calories 412.4
Cholesterol 0.0mg
Sodium 1202.0mg
Carbohydrates 71.5g
Protein 8.3g

Ingredients

3 tbsp olive oil
1 large onion, diced
6 garlic cloves, minced
1/2 tsp red chili pepper flakes
2 tsp salt
1 tbsp chili powder
1 tbsp sweet paprika
2 tsp oregano
1 large red pepper, chopped
1 large yellow pepper, chopped
4 medium tomatoes, ripe, chopped
1 1/4 C. arborio rice

3 C. hot vegetable stock
1/2 lb green beans, trimmed and sliced into 1 inch lengths
fresh ground pepper
1/2 bunch cilantro, chopped
1/2 bunch parsley, chopped
1 bunch scallion, minced
aged cheddar cheese or parmesan cheese

Directions

1. In a large pan, heat the oil and sauté the onion till tender.
2. Add the garlic, chili flakes and salt and sauté for a few minutes.
3. Stir in the tomatoes, peppers, herbs, spices and salt and simmer, covered for about 10 minutes.
4. Stir in the rice till it is coated with the mixture.
5. Add the hot broth and bring to a boil.
6. Reduce the heat to low and simmer, covered for about 30 minutes.
7. Meanwhile steam the green beans till the desired doneness.
8. Add the green beans, herbs and black pepper in the pan and stir to combine.
9. Serve with a garnishing of cheese and scallions.

Incredibly Delicious Paella

Prep Time: 45 mins
Total Time: 46 mins

Servings per Recipe: 6
Calories   668.6
Cholesterol   200.4mg
Sodium   1120.0mg
Carbohydrates   66.7g
Protein   47.3g

Ingredients

1 lb extra-large shrimp, peeled and deveined
salt and pepper
olive oil
2 tbsp garlic, minced
1 lb boneless skinless chicken thighs, trimmed of excess fat and halved crosswise
1 red bell pepper, seeded and cut pole to pole into 1/2-inch-wide strips
8 oz. chorizo sausage, Spanish sliced 1/2 inch thick on the bias
1 medium onion, chopped fine
1 (14 1/2 oz.) cans diced tomatoes, drained, minced, and drained again
2 C. arborio rice
3 C. low chicken broth
2/3 C. dry white wine
1/2 tsp saffron thread, crumbled
1 bay leaf
1/8 tsp dried thyme
paprika, as required
1 tsp ground cumin
1 dozen mussels, scrubbed and debearded
1/2 C. frozen green pea, thawed
2 tsp fresh parsley leaves, chopped
1 lemon, cut into wedges, for serving

Directions

1. Set your oven to 350 degrees F before doing anything else and arrange the oven rack to the lower-middle position.
2. In a bowl, add the shrimp, 1 tsp of the garlic, 1 tbsp of the oil, salt and black pepper and toss to coat well.
3. Refrigerate, covered till serving.
4. In another bowl, add the chicken and season with the salt and black pepper.
5. In a large Dutch oven, heat 2 tsp of the oil on medium-high heat and sauté the peppers for about 3-4 minutes.
6. Transfer the peppers onto a plate.

7. In the same pan, heat 1 tsp of the oil and cook the chicken for about 3 minutes per side.
8. Transfer the chicken into another plate.
9. Reduce the heat to medium and cook the chorizo for about 4-5 minutes.
10. Transfer the chorizo to the plate with the chicken.
11. In the same Dutch oven, heat 2 tbsp of the oil on medium heat and sauté the onion for about 3 minutes.
12. Add the remaining garlic and sauté for about 1 minute.
13. Add the tomatoes and cook for about 3 minutes.
14. Add the rice and stir fry for about 1-2 minutes.
15. Add the wine, broth, saffron, paprika, cumin, thyme, bay leaf and salt and bring to a boil on medium-high heat.
16. Cover and cook in the oven for about 30 minutes.
17. Stir in the chicken and chorizo, cover, and cook everything in the oven for about 15 minutes.
18. Insert the mussels into rice mixture, hinged side down and place the shrimp over the rice.
19. Top everything with the peppers, cover, and cook it in the oven for about 10-12 minutes.
20. Remove everything from the oven and keep it aside, covered, for about 5 minutes before serving.
21. Serve hot with a garnishing of parsley and lemon wedges.

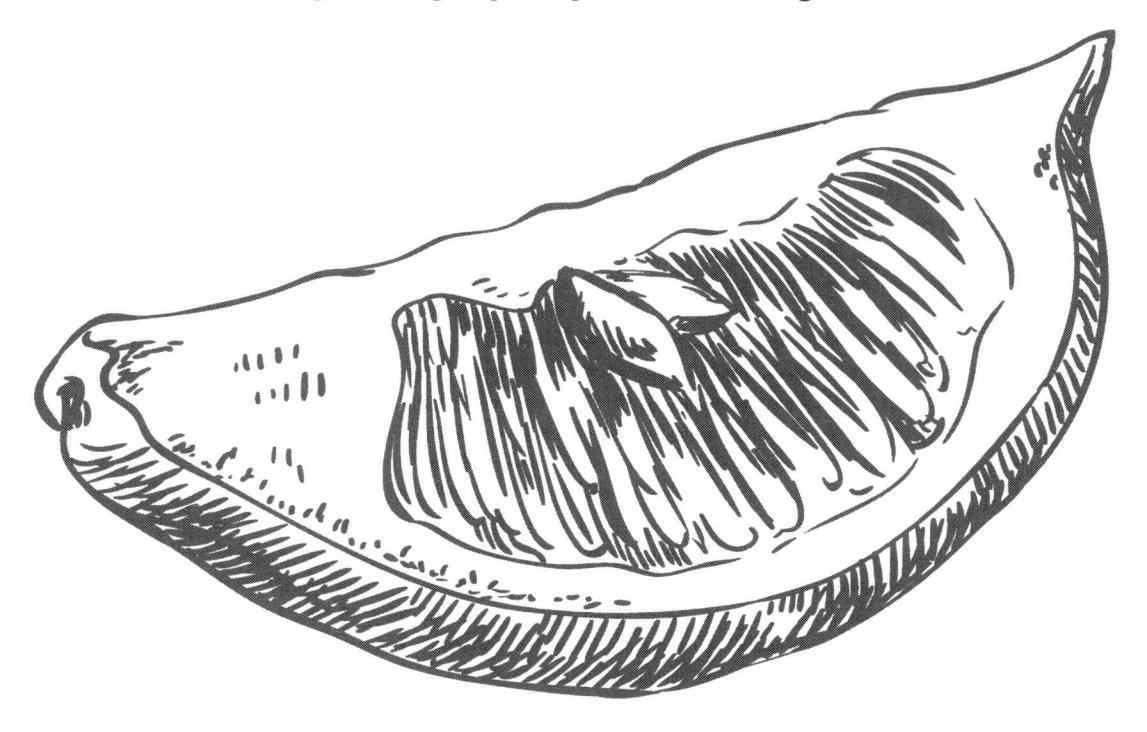

Gourmet Dinner Paella

Prep Time: 20 mins
Total Time: 30 mins

Servings per Recipe: 6
Calories   529.9
Cholesterol   66.5mg
Sodium   1459.3mg
Carbohydrates   37.7g
Protein   25.0g

Ingredients

1 lb chorizo sausage, removed from casings
1/2 C. onion, diced
2 garlic cloves, finely chopped
1 C. pumpkin, cooked
1/2 C. frozen peas
1/2 tsp cinnamon
1/2 tsp ground nutmeg
1/8 tsp ground cloves
fresh parsley
fresh snipped chives

Roasted Tomatoes
2 medium tomatoes, chopped
1 tbsp honey
drizzle olive oil
salt and pepper
Saffron Rice
4 C. chicken broth
1 pinch saffron thread
1 C. arborio rice

Directions

1. Set your oven to 325 degrees F before doing anything else and lightly grease a baking sheet.
2. For the roasted tomatoes, in a bowl, add the tomatoes, oil, honey, salt and black pepper and toss to coat.
3. Transfer the tomato mixture onto the prepared baking sheet and cook in the oven for about 20 minutes.
4. For the rice, in a pan, add the broth and bring to a boil.
5. Stir in the rice and saffron and bring to a boil.
6. Reduce the heat to low and simmer, covered for about 20 minutes.
7. For the paella, heat a large skillet on medium heat and stir fry the sausage, onion and garlic breaking the sausage into pieces.
8. Stir in the cooked rice, pumpkin, roasted tomatoes, peas and spices and simmer, covered for about 5-10 minutes. Serve hot with a garnishing of chives and parsley.

ISLAND
Chicken Paella

Prep Time: 25 mins
Total Time: 1 hr

Servings per Recipe: 4
Calories	648.2
Cholesterol	103.5mg
Sodium	829.8mg
Carbohydrates	50.6g
Protein	36.0g

Ingredients

2 -3 lb. chicken pieces
3 tbsp olive oil
salt and pepper
1 medium onion, sliced into thin wedges
2 tbsp fresh minced garlic
1 C. long-grain white rice, uncooked
1 (14 1/2 oz.) can diced tomatoes
3 C. chicken broth
2 tbsp capers
1 tsp cayenne pepper
12 Spanish olives, green with pimento, sliced
1 C. frozen peas, thawed
1 (7 oz.) jar roasted sweet peppers

Directions

1. In a large paella pan, heat the oil and cook the chicken with the salt and black pepper till browned from all the sides.
2. Transfer the chicken into a bowl.
3. In the same pan, sauté the onion and garlic till tender.
4. Stir in the rice and stir fry for about 1 minute.
5. Stir in the cooked chicken, tomatoes, capers, cayenne pepper and broth and bring to a boil.
6. Reduce the heat to very low and simmer, covered for about 30-40 minutes.
7. Gently, fold in the peas and olives and top with the pepper strips.
8. Simmer, covered for about 3-4 minutes.

South African Style Paella

Prep Time: 15 mins
Total Time: 2 hrs 15 mins

Servings per Recipe: 6
Calories   951.0
Cholesterol   336.8mg
Sodium   984.6mg
Carbohydrates   80.4g
Protein   81.4g

Ingredients

- 1/4 C. cooking oil
- 3 red sweet peppers, julienned
- 1 large onion, chopped
- 1 lb pork, cubed
- 5 chicken thighs, halved
- 4 C. boiling water
- 1 tsp saffron
- 4 bay leaves
- 2 chicken stock cubes
- 2 lb. kingklip or white perch fillets, cut in strips
- 12 oz. prawns, frozen
- 1 lb rice, uncooked
- salt and pepper
- 8 oz. frozen green peas
- 1 lemon, juice of

Directions

1. In a pan, heat the oil and sauté the chicken, pork, onion and pepper till golden brown.
2. Reduce the heat to very low and simmer, covered for about 1 hour.
3. In a bowl, mix together the boiling water, chicken cubes, saffron and bay leaves.
4. Uncover the pan and place the seafood over the meat mixture.
5. Top everything with the rice and peas and season the dish with the salt and black pepper.
6. Slowly, add the water mixture and cook till all the liquid is absorbed.
7. Stir in the lemon juice and serve.

PERSIAN
Paella

Prep Time: 20 mins
Total Time: 20 mins

Servings per Recipe: 2
Calories	435.3
Cholesterol	28.3mg
Sodium	1260.5mg
Carbohydrates	30.5g
Protein	14.8g

Ingredients

- 1 pinch saffron
- 2 tbsp lemon juice
- 2 tbsp olive oil
- 1 tsp agave syrup
- 1 dash sea salt
- 1/2 C. shitake mushrooms
- 1/2 C. water
- 1/4 C. rice wine vinegar
- 2 tbsp soy sauce
- 1 tbsp dulse flakes
- 1 tsp paprika
- Paella Rice
- 1 1/2 C. turnips, chopped
- 1/3 C. pine nuts
- 1/4 C. bell pepper
- 2 tbsp onions
- 1 tsp garlic
- 2 small tomatoes, chopped
- 1/2 C. fresh peas
- 1/4 C. parsley
- 1/4 C. sun-dried tomato, soaked well chopped

Directions

1. For the dressing, in a bowl, soak the saffron in lemon juice for about 20 minutes.
2. Add the remaining dressing ingredients and stir to combine.
3. Meanwhile in a large bowl, mix together all the mushroom marinate ingredients.
4. In a food processor, add the bell peppers, turnips, onion, garlic and pine nuts and pulse till a rice like consistency forms.
5. Drain the mushrooms from the marinade.
6. Transfer the veggie mixture into a bowl with the tomatoes, peas, parsley and dressing and stir to combine.
7. Top the salad with the mushrooms and green olives.
8. Serve the salad with a sprinkling of paprika.

Innovative Paella

🥣 Prep Time: 20 mins
⏱ Total Time: 50 mins

Servings per Recipe: 6
Calories   393.2
Cholesterol   26.1mg
Sodium   539.4mg
Carbohydrates   51.9g
Protein   21.5g

Ingredients

1/4 C. olive oil
16 oz. scallops
1 large onion, chopped
2 garlic cloves, minced
1 1/2 C. rice
3 1/4 C. fish stock
1/4 tsp saffron
salt and pepper
1 red bell pepper, roasted and cut in strips

18 mild green canned chilies
1 (14 oz.) can artichoke hearts, drained and sprinkled with lemon juice
lemon wedge

Directions

1. In a paella pan, heat half of the oil on medium-high heat and sauté the scallops for about 3 minutes.
2. Transfer the scallops in a bowl and remove the pan liquid.
3. In the same pan, heat the remaining oil on medium heat and sauté the onion and garlic for about 5 minutes.
4. Stir in the rice and stir fry for about 5 minutes.
5. Stir in the saffron, salt, black pepper and broth and simmer for about 10 minutes.
6. Stir in the scallops and artichoke and simmer for about 5 minutes.
7. Serve hot with a garnishing of lemon wedges and extra roasted bell pepper strips.

PAELLA
for Parties

Prep Time: 20 mins
Total Time: 50 mins

Servings per Recipe: 2
Calories   400.9
Cholesterol   61.8mg
Sodium   928.6mg
Carbohydrates   9.9g
Protein   22.9g

Ingredients

2 C. chicken broth
3/4 C. dry white wine
1/2 tsp saffron thread
3 tbsp olive oil
6 oz. thin spaghetti, broken into 2-inch lengths
6 large shrimp, shelled
6 large sea scallops
6 clams, scrubbed

4 oz. frozen artichoke hearts, thawed
1 tsp chives

Directions

1. Set your oven to 400 degrees F before doing anything else and arrange a rack in the middle of the oven.
2. In a pan, heat the broth and wine and stir in the saffron.
3. Keep the pan on low heat.
4. In an ovenproof skillet, heat the oil on medium-high heat and stir fry the pasta for about 2 minutes.
5. Add the hot broth and simmer for about 5 minutes.
6. Insert the seafood into the pasta mixture and cook the mix in the oven for about 20 minutes.
7. Serve hot with a garnishing of chives.

Italian Paella

Prep Time: 10 mins
Total Time: 45 mins

Servings per Recipe: 2
Calories	677.2
Cholesterol	47.3mg
Sodium	1016.1mg
Carbohydrates	74.6g
Protein	22.4g

Ingredients

- 2 Italian sausages, removed from casing
- 1/2 red bell pepper, 1/2-inch strips
- 1/2 green bell pepper, 1/2-inch strips
- 1 small onion, 1/2-inch wedges
- 1/2 tbsp olive oil
- 3/4 C. arborio rice
- 1/2 C. dry white wine
- 1 C. tomatoes, canned, drained
- 1 1/2 C. water

Directions

1. Set your oven to 400 degrees F before doing anything else.
2. In an ovenproof skillet, heat the oil and stir fry the sausage, onion and bell peppers for about 5 minutes.
3. Stir in the rice and stir fry for about 1 minute.
4. Stir in the remaining ingredients and bring to a boil.
5. Now, cook in the oven for about 25 minutes.
6. Season with the salt and black pepper and serve.

PALEO
Paella

🍳 Prep Time: 15 mins
🕐 Total Time: 45 mins

Servings per Recipe: 4
Calories   454.6
Cholesterol   100.2mg
Sodium   1451.0mg
Carbohydrates   12.8g
Protein   33.6g

Ingredients

10 oz. chorizo sausage
2 boneless skinless chicken breasts, cut into bite-size pieces
1 tsp paprika
1 tsp cumin
1/2 tsp salt
1/2 tsp pepper
1 medium onion, sliced
1 red pepper, sliced

1 large tomatoes, sliced
3 garlic cloves, minced fine
1 pinch saffron
1 C. chicken broth
1/2 head cauliflower, grated with box grater (to resemble rice)

Directions

1. In a large pan, cook the chorizo till browned.
2. Transfer the chorizo to a plate, leaving the fat in the pan.
3. In the same pan, cook the chicken with the cumin, paprika, salt and black pepper and cook till done completely.
4. Stir in the pepper and onion and cook till tender.
5. Stir in the tomatoes, garlic, salt and black pepper and cook, stirring occasionally till a thick mixture forms.
6. Add the saffron and broth and cook, stirring continuously till all the liquid is absorbed.
7. Stir in the remaining ingredients and cook the paella until everything is fully done.
8. Place the dish in the oven for 10 mins at 350 degrees then let the dish set in the oven for 10 more mins.

Paella in Barcelona Style

Prep Time: 5 mins
Total Time: 1 hr 5 mins

Servings per Recipe: 3
Calories	2255.4
Cholesterol	655.0mg
Sodium	662.9mg
Carbohydrates	119.9g
Protein	166.4g

Ingredients

- 4 C. water
- 1/2 C. dry white wine
- 2 tbsp black tea
- 1 tbsp oil
- 1 C. snow peas
- 1 C. water chestnut
- 1 red chili
- 1 onion (finely chopped)
- 2 C. rice
- 1 C. dried mango
- 1 kg chicken drumstick

Directions

1. In a large paella pan, heat the oil and stir fry the chicken till golden brown.
2. Stir in the mangos, onion and chili and cook, stirring occasionally for a few minutes.
3. Stir in the rice, tea and 2 C. of the water and cook, stirring occasionally till most of the liquid is absorbed.
4. Add the remaining 2 C. of the water and cook, stirring occasionally till all the liquid is absorbed.
5. Add the wine and cook till all the liquid is absorbed.
6. Stir in the peas and water chestnut and cook till the veggies are heated completely.

DENVER STYLE
Paella

Prep Time: 10 mins
Total Time: 40 mins

Servings per Recipe: 4
Calories 559.0
Cholesterol 161.5mg
Sodium 1166.4mg
Carbohydrates 62.0g
Protein 37.4g

Ingredients

1 tbsp olive oil
1/2 C. onion, chopped
6 oz. chicken sausage, cooked and thinly sliced
2 (3 1/2 oz.) packages brown rice (boil-in-bag)
salt
1/2 tsp smoked paprika
1/4 tsp black pepper

1 (15 oz.) can chicken broth
1 (14 1/2 oz.) can diced tomatoes, undrained
2 tsp garlic, minced
1 1/2 C. edamame, frozen. shelled
1/4 tsp saffron thread
1/2 lb frozen shrimp, thawed

Directions

1. In a large pan, heat the oil on medium-high heat and sauté the sausage and onion till the onions become tender.
2. Stir in the rice, paprika, salt and black pepper and sauté for about 30 seconds.
3. Add the tomatoes, garlic and broth and bring to a boil.
4. Reduce the heat to medium and simmer, covered for about 10 minutes.
5. Stir in the remaining ingredients and simmer for about 4 minutes.

Fiesta Paella

Prep Time: 30 mins
Total Time: 30 mins

Servings per Recipe: 4
Calories	1337.3
Cholesterol	415.8mg
Sodium	1105.0mg
Carbohydrates	122.6g
Protein	88.6g

Ingredients

- 1/4 C. oil
- 1/4 kg pork
- 3 garlic cloves
- 1/2 chopped onion
- 1 tbsp tomato puree
- 1/2 kg rice
- 1/2 kg shrimp, shelled
- 1/2 chicken
- 100 g chorizo sausage
- 3 green peppers, sliced
- 1 C. peas
- 1 bay leaf
- salt and pepper
- 1 liter water
- 2 links chopped pork sausage
- 1/2 C. squid, chopped
- 1/2 C. crawfish, chopped
- 3 artichoke hearts
- 1/4 kg cockles

Directions

1. In a pan of water, boil the cockles till the shells are opened and reserve the cooking water.
2. In a large skillet, heat the oil and stir fry all the ingredients except the rice and cockles.
3. Add the rice and stir fry till all the liquid is absorbed.
4. Add enough reserved cooking water and bring to a boil.
5. Simmer till the mixture becomes thick.
6. Stir in the cockles and place the pan over a hot plate and cook till the rice is done.
7. Remove everything from the heat and keep aside, covered for about 20 minutes before serving.

NUTRITIOUS Paella

Prep Time: 30 mins
Total Time: 1 hr

Servings per Recipe: 6
Calories   406.0
Cholesterol   0.0mg
Sodium   194.3mg
Carbohydrates   72.7g
Protein   9.3g

Ingredients

1/4 C. olive oil
5 minced garlic cloves
1 large yellow onion, chopped
4 C. vegetable broth
2 C. rice (uncooked)
4 medium tomatoes, skinned, seeded and chopped
1 small red bell pepper, seeded and cut into thin strips
1 small green bell pepper, seeded and cut into thin strips
1 small yellow bell pepper, seeded and cut into thin strips
1 C. green peas
2 C. artichoke hearts, tough outer leaves removed and quartered
1 lemon
lemon wedge, to garnish

Directions

1. In a pan, heat the broth.
2. In a large paella pan, heat the oil and sauté the onion and garlic till tender.
3. Add the rice and stir fry for about 3 minutes.
4. Stir in the tomatoes and bell pepper and stir fry for about 3 minutes.
5. Add the hot broth and simmer on medium heat for about 20 minutes.
6. Stir in the peas, artichoke and lemon juice and remove everything from the heat.
7. Serve hot with a garnishing of lemon wedges.

Hearty Paella

Prep Time: 10 mins
Total Time: 40 mins

Servings per Recipe: 8
Calories   154.0
Cholesterol   88.9mg
Sodium   580.0mg
Carbohydrates   5.8g
Protein   12.6g

Ingredients

- 2 C. water
- 1/2 lb smoked sausage, halved lengthwise and sliced 1/4-inch thick
- 1 (14 1/2 oz.) cans diced tomatoes, undrained
- 1/2 C. chopped onion
- 1 tsp dried parsley flakes
- 1 (7 oz.) packages Yellow Rice
- 1 lb large shrimp, peeled and deveined
- 1 C. frozen peas

Directions

1. In a large skillet, mix together the sausage, onion, tomato, parsley and water and bring to a boil.
2. Stir in the rice mix and reduce the heat to low.
3. Simmer, covered for about 15 minutes.
4. Stir in the peas and shrimp and simmer, covered for about 10-15 minutes, stirring occasionally.
5. Remove everything from the heat and keep aside, covered for about 5 minutes before serving.

PAELLA
in Vegan Style

Prep Time: 20 mins
Total Time: 55 mins

Servings per Recipe: 6
Calories   269.6
Cholesterol   0.0mg
Sodium   260.0mg
Carbohydrates   42.1g
Protein   9.0g

Ingredients

1 pinch saffron thread
2 C. vegetable broth
1/2 C. water
4 vegetarian sausages, cut into 1-inch pieces
1 tbsp olive oil, for drizzling
1 large onion, chopped
salt and pepper

1/4 C. chopped pimiento
1 C. frozen peas
1/3 C. dry sherry
3 tbsp vegan margarine
1/2 C. orzo pasta
1 C. brown rice
1/2 C. flat leaf parsley, chopped

Directions

1. In a pan, mix together 2 C. of the broth, 1/2 C. of the water and saffron on medium heat and bring to a boil.
2. Reduce the heat to low and keep covered for a few minutes.
3. In a skillet, heat a little oil on medium-high heat and cook the sausage for about 2-3 minutes.
4. Transfer the sausage into a bowl.
5. In the same skillet, heat a little oil more and sauté the onion, salt and black pepper for about 3 minutes.
6. Stir in the peas, pimentos and sherry and cook, stirring for about 1-2 minutes and transfer onto a plate.
7. In the same skillet, melt 2 tbsp of the margarine on medium heat and cook the pasta for about 3-4 minutes.
8. Add the broth mixture and rice and bring to a boil.
9. Reduce the heat to low and simmer, covered for about 18 minutes.
10. Meanwhile set your oven to 375 degrees F and grease a casserole dish with the remaining melted margarine.

11. Transfer the rice mixture into the prepared casserole dish evenly and top with the onion mixture and sausage.
12. Cover the casserole dish loosely and cook in the oven for about 20 minutes.
13. Uncover and cook in the oven for about 10 minutes more.
14. Serve hot with a garnishing of parsley.

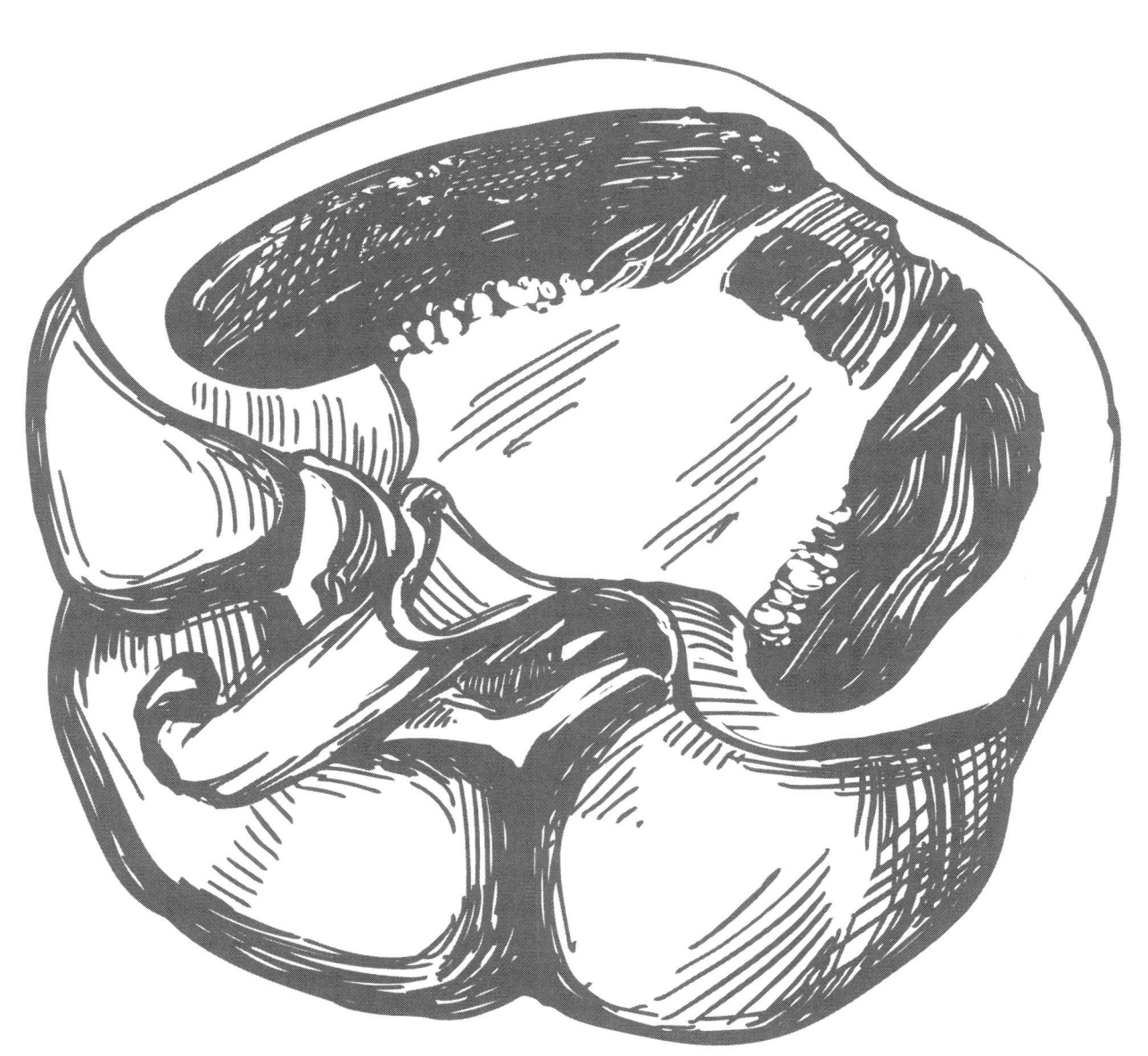

FAMILY FRIENDLY
Paella

Prep Time: 10 mins
Total Time: 40 mins

Servings per Recipe: 4
Calories 551.8
Cholesterol 0.0mg
Sodium 47.8mg
Carbohydrates 91.1g
Protein 8.6g

Ingredients

3 C. water
1/2 C. white wine
1 1/2 lb. ripe tomatoes, cored and cut into thick wedges
salt & freshly ground black pepper
1/4 C. extra virgin olive oil
1 medium onion, minced
1 tbsp minced garlic

1 tbsp tomato paste
1 pinch saffron thread
1 - 2 tsp paprika
2 C. short-grain rice
minced parsley, and basil (to garnish)

Directions

1. Set your oven to 450 degrees F before doing anything else.
2. In a pan, warm the water.
3. In a bowl, add the tomatoes, 1 tbsp of the oil salt and black pepper and toss to coat well.
4. In a 12-inch ovenproof skillet, heat the remaining oil on medium-high heat and sauté the bell pepper, onion, garlic, salt and black pepper for about 3-5 minutes.
5. Stir in the tomato paste, saffron and paprika and sauté for about 1 minute.
6. Add the rice and stir fry for about 1-2 minutes.
7. Add the wine and cook till all the liquid is absorbed then stir in the hot water.
8. Place the tomato mixture over the rice mixture and cook in the oven for about 15 minutes.
9. If rice is dry and not done completely, then add the required amount of broth and cook everything in the oven for about 5-10 mins more.
10. Turn off the oven but keep the pan inside for about 5-15 minutes before serving.
11. Serve with a topping of the basil and parsley.

Flavor-Packed Paella

Prep Time: 15 mins
Total Time: 5 hrs 15 mins

Servings per Recipe: 4
Calories   1227.5
Cholesterol   302.7mg
Sodium   1008.2mg
Carbohydrates   56.0g
Protein   83.4g

Ingredients

- 3 lb. chicken, chopped into medium chunks
- 1 tbsp olive oil
- 8 oz. cooked sausage, sliced
- 1 onion, sliced
- 3 tsp garlic, minced
- 2 tsp dried thyme
- 1 1/4 tsp pepper
- 1 tsp paprika
- 1/8 tsp saffron
- 1/2 tsp turmeric
- 14 1/2 oz. chicken broth
- 1/2 C. water
- 2 yellow peppers, diced
- 1 C. green peas
- 3 C. cooked rice

Directions

1. In a large pan, heat the oil and stir fry the chicken till golden brown.
2. Drain the excess fat and transfer the chicken into the slow cooker with sausage, onion, garlic, saffron, thyme and spices.
3. Pour the water and broth and set the slow cooker on low settings.
4. Cover and cook for about 8 hours.
5. Uncover the slow cooker and immediately, stir in the peas, tomatoes and peppers.
6. Serve the chicken mixture over the rice.

VERSATILE
Paella

Prep Time: 20 mins
Total Time: 24 mins

Servings per Recipe: 6
Calories 307.8
Cholesterol 108.5mg
Sodium 1013.0mg
Carbohydrates 18.2g
Protein 20.7g

Ingredients

1 tbsp vegetable oil
1 lb chicken sausage, sliced diagonally
1 small onion, finely chopped
2 garlic cloves, finely chopped
1 red bell pepper, unseeded, cut into strips
4 C. low chicken broth
1 (14 oz.) cans diced tomatoes
1 (16 oz.) packages Spanish rice mix
4 oz. cooked ham, chopped
1 C. frozen peas
salt

Directions

1. In a large skillet, heat 1 tbsp of the oil on medium-high heat and cook the sausage for about 5 minutes.
2. Transfer the sausage into a slow cooker.
3. In the same skillet, sauté the onion, bell pepper and garlic for about 3-5 minutes and transfer into the slow cooker.
4. In the same skillet, add 1 cup of the broth on high heat and bring to a boil, stirring continuously and pour into a slow cooker.
5. Add the remaining ingredients except the peas and set the slow cooker on low.
6. Cover and cook for about 4 hours.
7. Uncover the slow cooker and stir in the peas and cook, covered for about 15 minutes more.

Traditional Restaurant Style Paella

Prep Time: 10 mins
Total Time: 1 hr

Servings per Recipe: 4
Calories   747.9
Cholesterol   0.0mg
Sodium   91.4mg
Carbohydrates   136.8g
Protein   17.5g

Ingredients

- 1/4 C. olive oil
- 1/2 C. onion, chopped
- 1 tsp garlic, finely chopped
- 1 medium-size sweet red peppers or 1 green pepper, seeded, deribbed and cut into strips
- 8 pieces asparagus
- 1 tomatoes, chopped
- 1/2 C. fresh peas
- 1/2 tsp saffron, ground
- 8 medium-size mushrooms, sliced
- salt & pepper
- 2 artichokes, cut in quarters
- 6 C. boiling water
- 3 C. medium grain rice

Directions

1. Set your oven to 400 degrees F before doing anything else.
2. In a large deep ovenproof skillet, heat the oil on medium heat and stir fry the vegetables for about 1 minute.
3. Stir in the rice, salt, black pepper and water and bring to a boil.
4. Stir in the saffron and arrange the skillet on the floor of the oven.
5. Cook for about 20 minutes.
6. Remove from the oven and keep aside, covered for about 5 minutes before serving.

COMFORT brown Rice Paella

Prep Time: 20 mins
Total Time: 1 hr 8 mins

Servings per Recipe: 6
Calories 747.5
Cholesterol 220.7mg
Sodium 933.3mg
Carbohydrates 64.3g
Protein 50.6g

Ingredients

1 lb extra-large shrimp, peeled and deveined
salt & freshly ground black pepper
olive oil
8 -9 medium garlic cloves
1 lb chicken thigh
1 red bell pepper, seeded and cut pole to pole into 1/2-inch-wide strips
8 oz. spanish chorizo, sliced 1/2 inch thick on the bias
1 medium onion, chopped fine
1 (14 1/2 oz.) cans diced tomatoes, drained, minced, and drained again

2 C. long grain brown rice
3 C. low chicken broth
1/3 C. dry white wine
1/2 tsp saffron thread, crumbled
1 bay leaf
1 dozen mussels, scrubbed and debearded
1/2 C. frozen green pea, thawed
2 tsp fresh parsley leaves
1 lemon, cut into wedges, for serving

Directions

1. Set your oven to 350 degrees F before doing anything else and arrange the oven rack to lower-middle position.
2. In s bowl, add the shrimp, 1 tsp of the garlic, 1 tbsp of the oil, salt and black pepper and toss to coat well.
3. Refrigerate, covered till serving.
4. In another bowl, add the chicken and season with the salt and black pepper.
5. In a large Dutch oven, heat 2 tsp of the oil on medium-high heat and sauté the peppers for about 3-4 minutes.
6. Transfer the peppers into a plate.
7. In the same pan, heat 1 tsp of the oil and cook the chicken for about 3 minutes.
8. Transfer the chicken into another plate.

9. Reduce the heat to medium and cook the chorizo for about 4-5 minutes.
10. Transfer the chorizo in the plate with the chicken.
11. In the same Dutch oven, heat 2 tbsp of the oil on medium heat and sauté the onion for about 3 minutes.
12. Add the remaining garlic and sauté for about 1 minute.
13. Add the tomatoes and cook for about 3 minutes.
14. Add the rice and stir fry for about 1-2 minutes.
15. Add the wine, broth, saffron, bay leaf and salt and bring to a boil on medium-high heat.
16. Cover and cook in the oven for about 30 minutes.
17. Stir in the chicken and chorizo, cover and cook in the oven for about 15 minutes.
18. Insert the mussels in rice mixture, hinged side down and place the shrimp over rice.
19. Top with the peppers, cover and cook in the oven for about 12 minutes.
20. Remove from the oven and keep aside, covered for about 5 minutes before serving.
21. Serve hot with a garnishing of parsley and lemon wedges.

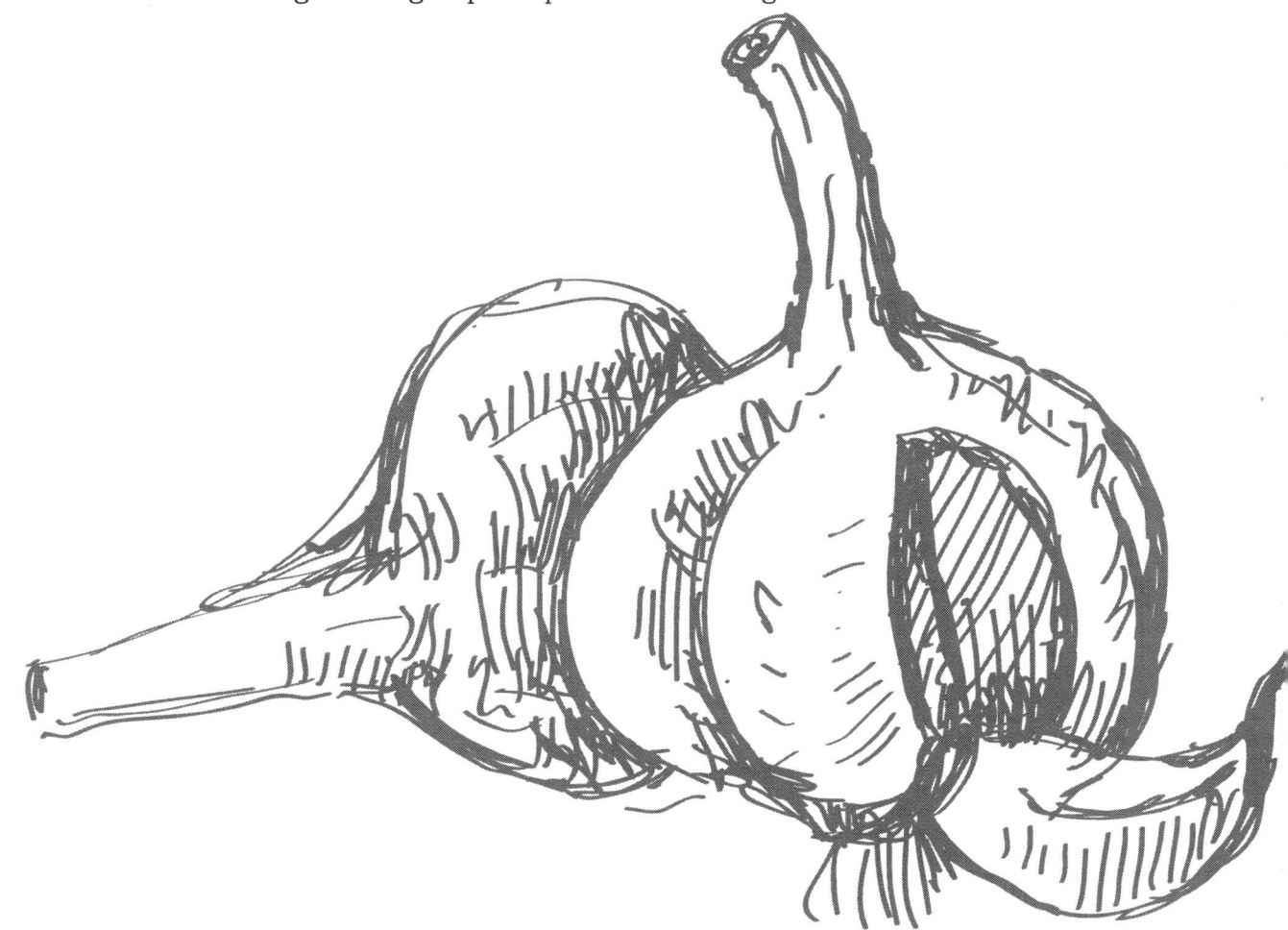

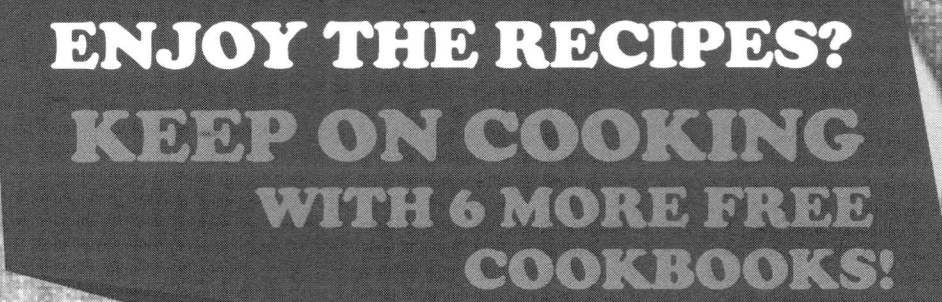

ENJOY THE RECIPES?
KEEP ON COOKING WITH 6 MORE FREE COOKBOOKS!

Visit our website and simply enter your email address to join the club and receive your 6 cookbooks.

http://booksumo.com/magnet

https://www.instagram.com/booksumopress/

https://www.facebook.com/booksumo/

Printed in Great Britain
by Amazon